Kyra Belán

Kyra Belán: From Myth to Reality

Kyra Belán

Ceres Gallery

547 W 27th St #201,
New York, NY 10001

Kyra Belán: From Myth to Reality
April 2 - 27, 2019

Ceres Gallery, 547 W 27th St #201, New York, NY 10001

Cover design: Kyra Belán, Charles Martin
Front cover art: E.R.A. NOW copyright Kyra Belán 2018
Catalog design: Kyra Belán
Back cover photograph: Charles Martin Photography

www.kyrabelan.com

ISBN-9781097634729

Astarte Books 2019

Contents

Foreword 6
Kyra Belán

Acknowledgments 7
Kyra Belán

From Myth to Reality 8
Kyra Belán

Interpreting Legends, Inspiring Leadership 10
Alessandra Comini

Amazing Women: Divine to Reality 11
Carol Damian, Ph.D.
Art Historian

Hopeful Resistance toward Social Transformation 12
Basia Sliwinska
Senior Lecturer in Cultural and Historical Studies,
University of the Arts, London

Installation Views 14

Individual Art Works 16

List of Works 36

Curriculum Vitae (Selected) 38

Selected You Tube Videos 57

Bio Sketch 58

Foreword

From Myth to Reality, my solo exhibition at Ceres Gallery in New York, was concieved to be about the fact that in 2019 women still do not have equal rights, are paid lower wages than men and are treated as second class citizens. Our country, which used to be a democracy, is rapidly being transformed into an oligarchy. The White House and the Senate are in the hands of powerful men that are modeling their behavior after other plutocratic regimes, and numerous judges that are being appointed by the president are not adhering to the constitutional principles of a democratic society. Currently the cards are stacked in favor of the wealthy and privileged class of usually white and often old males. My hope is that my art will encourage the voters to elect women and "We the People", the humanity that inhabits this wonderful country in demographic proportions that match our constituency.

My choice of Ceres Gallery for this solo exhibition is most appropriate. I accepted the invitation due to the fact that Ceres Gallery is the only feminist gallery not only in Chelsea but also in Manhattan. I wanted a space that would not dictate or constrict my artistic expression, as it is usually the case with other venues and is often something that female artists, who are seriously discriminated against in every aspect of their professional journey have to tolerate and abide by. For decades I have been censored while exhibiting my artworks due to the fact that my subject matter did not conform to the patriarchal rules devised exclusively for women.

The historical face of Ceres Gallery includes its founding in 1984 as a part of the New York Feminist Art Institute (1979-1990), several relocations on Manhattan, and its current location at the Landmark Arts Building in Chelsea, New York. The Gallery functions as a feminist cultural and educational center and, besides the year round exhibition schedule at their two galleries, presents events, art projects, political arts, and celebrates Women's History Month.

Kyra Belán

Acknowledgments

My sincere thanks go to the president of Ceres Gallery, Susan Grabel, and the gallery director Stefany Benson, without whose help this exhibition could not have taken place. My deep gratitude goes to the amazing artist and curator Regina Corritore, without whose skillful help of arranging and hanging this exhibition this event could not have materialized. My sincere thanks to Crumlic Media for the video of this exhibit. Many thanks to the staff of Michi's Art and Frame, Fort Myers, for the excellent matting and framing of the artworks featured in this exhibition; and Lorne Art Gallery, Cape Coral, for crating the artworks.

My deep gratitude goes to the art historians who wrote the essays for this catalog: the renown author and art historian Carol Damian, and the amazing cultural historian and author Basia Sliwinska. Lastly, my gratitude to the prolific and celebrated art historian, author, musicologist, and murder mystery writer, Alessandra Comini.

Kyra Belán

Kyra Belán: From Myth to Reality

Artist's Statement

Since the beginning of my long career as an artist I have been interested in female centered myths and symbols through time and the stories of real women and their incredible contributions to our civilization. Women mold our society in all areas of life. This includes spirituality, arts, and politics. Yet women are undervalued by current patriarchal societies. I believe that women are the key to the future of our civilization, and focusing on women's contributions to our culture helps and improves our social order. For this exhibition I chose to concentrate on painting, drawing, and mixed media installation. For the last two years I have been developing my Lady Liberty Series that feature this universal symbol for Democracy. The Lady has a long history of divine descent from the old matriarchal cultures of ancient Europe and the world that worshiped Mother God. She connects us to the great matriarchal civilization of the island of Crete, as well as to the Goddess Athena of the Greeks and the Goddess of Liberty of the Ancient Rome. The statue of Liberty today is a world - wide symbol for freedom and democracy, and also functions as an American symbol for the rights of The People.

The women celebrated in this exhibition include great visual artists, writers, and politicians. Since these fields are discriminatory to women in multiple ways, I feel that it is urgent for women to keep fighting for their right to equal representation as members within our democratic society. Because of the deep misogyny of our current patriarchal culture we have a long way to go because the mental chains of oppression are as extensive as the physical. Women must liberate their minds from the deeply ingrained sexist thinking in order to be equal to men. I see the new millennium as a crucial time-space in which women can and will gain their equality.

In 2016, Hilary Clinton won her presidential election by popular vote, only to lose to her opponent because of the Electoral College voters. Clinton's saying, "women's rights are human rights, once and for all," is a promise, not a fact. Chinese leader Mao Zedong once said that women hold up half the sky - a great saying, although in China women, as in the US, have never held top leadership positions like his.

The world will be a much better place for all when women will occupy as many leadership positions as men, and the revolution against patriarchy will gain momentum in the near future. Meanwhile, as my series of works evolve, I hope to continue contributing to the empowerment of women. The feminist majority will transform our culture into an eco-conscious society that will protect and preserve the environment.

Kyra Belán

Kyra Belán: Interpreting Legends, Inspiring Leadership

To look at a Belán image, whether it invokes an inspiring mythical figure or offers us an admired real-life person, past or present, is to enter a world of immediately recognizable figures who intrigue or inspire or perhaps even irk us, but through Belán's eyes, challenge us.

One of America's most established and admired artists, Belán has lately reintroduced us to an American icon: France's gift to America in 1886 of a statue commemorating the centennial of the American Declaration of Independence. Its title declares what it represents: Liberty Enlightening the World. When we see her through Belán's scope, we see the 151-foot-tall Lady Liberty's power to urge or commemorate relevant causes such as passage of the languishing equal rights amendment and the world-wide woman's march of 2017. We know Belán's powerhouse Lady, shown from so many different angles, will be there for future just causes as well. And Belán's Lady is a partisan. She is unabashedly focused on equality of the sexes. Yes, women and men are different, but yes they must stand on the same plane, equal under the law in politics, religion, health, sexual identity, education, employment, and opportunity.

As for her mighty personages, whether in the company of Lady Liberty or alone, whether living or deceased, Belán compels the viewer to think anew about them and their relationship to the Now we all experience. We are intrigued to be re-introduced to Hillary Clinton, Ruth Bader Ginsberg, Anita Hill, Maxine Waters, and Nancy Pelosi—ah, so many memories, so many events. What a pleasure to be reminded of Georgia O' Keeffe, Louise Bourgeois, Camille Claudel, Edmonia Lewis, and Frida Kahlo—artists, creators who just happened to be born female.

As an art historian who was once portrayed by Belán with an attribute referring to my work—a long book on the changing image of Beethoven—I realize that there is only one thing missing from this current exhibition: a self-image by the artist. As the proud owner of a Belán self-portrait, I can assure the reader that the world has been enriched by this committed artist who with the tools of colored pencil, watercolor, paint, and mixed media, brings us to the frontline of our lives.

Alessandra Comini

Kyra Belán: Amazing Women: Divine to Reality

It has been a life-long mission of Kyra Belán to create art in celebration of the female spirit, from the divine goddesses of ancient matriarchal civilizations, to the iconic image of the Statue of Liberty, to those of everyday women in history who have long fought for recognition and respect. Working in a wide range of media, she uses a repertoire of symbols to tell their stories in a unique style that is both recognizable and direct. With a pop-art sensibility, her technique reduces essential imagery to the most straightforward expression of character and personality, with a colorful palette for added interest and to project a dynamic energy to the message associated with each of their accomplishments. She captures more than the physical description of each subject; she reveals an inward sense of accomplishment, confidence and intellect. The amazing women in each work are meant to inspire and empower, as they bring much-needed attention to issues of discrimination, gender inequality, and lack of representation throughout history. Women have triumphed through the ages, inspired by the earliest belief systems which elevated them to the status of goddesses in a universal quest for fertility and beneficence built upon love and compassion. Women today still have that power, although their personal triumphs and acceptance in the modern world may appear to have little to do with the rituals of the past – they are the inheritors. The portraits reveal strength of character and the human spirit that have motivated each woman and given them the will to continue fighting their battles and delivering their messages, against the odds they continually face in a world not always prepared to recognize their success. Often imbued with political overtones, her works have a sense of immediacy that is accessible and clear, with no need for the caustic rhetoric that so often accompanies the faces of her strong personalities as they argue for their rights and the rights of others. Kyra Belán delivers a message of hope and optimism.

Carol Damian, Ph.D.
Art Historian
Miami, Florida

Hopeful Resistance toward Social Transformation

'The workshop of the future requires many hands and hearts. [...]
Proletarian women, the poorest of the poor, the most disempowered of
the disempowered, hurry to join the struggle for the emancipation of
women and of humankind from the horrors of capitalist domination!
Social Democracy has assigned to you a place of honor. Hurry to the front
lines, into the trenches!'
Rosa Luxemburg (2006) Reform and Revolution
and Other Writings, p. 245

Rosa Luxemburg, a writer and an activist, believed in and fought for
collective action. Her early twentieth century political activism and a
strong commitment to democracy and revolutionary mass action was
needed then, and is still much needed now, in times of thriving late
capitalism and neo-liberalism, populism, restrictions of civil liberties
and rising xenophobic rhetoric. This coincided with Donald Trump's
ascension to the White House in 2016, which encouraged further
economisation of everyday life and, more worryingly, the economization
of American racism furthering the fear of cultural differences. 2020 marks
the 100th anniversary of the ratification of the 19th amendment in the
united States, guaranteeing and protecting women's constitutional right
to vote. Next US presidential election is also scheduled for the year 2020.
This is an urgent time to call for collective action yet again.

   Kyra Belán's exhibition entitled From Myth to Reality at Ceres Gallery
in New York (2019) is an act of resistance and militancy through creative
art practice but also an expression of hope. Her artistic sensibilities are
informed by feminist agenda and support for women's suffrage. She
references and expands feminist 1970s activism and actions aimed at
consciousness raising. Belán calls for political and social transformation,
and a democratic renewal. Her paintings give women voice, encourage
them to talk about the dangers of the times we live in and remind us what
feminism stands for. Through depictions and engagement with female
centered myths and symbols, such as the figure of Libertas, the Roman
goddess and embodiment of liberty, Belán portrays stories of real women,
their contributions to our civilization and struggle for emancipation envis-
aged by Luxemburg. This painted and drawn 'workshop of the future' is
informed by care economy, return to ethical being in the world and belief
in communities, and justice.

Belán's disruptive visions create openings and possibilities to see the unseen, unhide the hidden and act. Paintings included in the exhibition are a form of manifestation and intervention forging a new language for feminism. Since 2013 Belán has been developing Lady Liberty Series that feature Lady Liberty, a universal symbol for democracy but also a world in which Mother God was celebrated. Her figure is juxtaposed with images of women including politicians, visual artists and writers. Belán reminds us of matriarchal ancient civilizations and calls for women to claim their place in the world and fight for human rights. She encourages women to intervene into and unsettle reproduced power structures and fight for democratic freedoms, equality and better political futures. The personal is crucial here. Similarly to Luxemburg, Belán calls for a collective action, and a rebuilding of the world. To quote Sara Ahmed, 'I think of feminism as a building project: if our texts are worlds, they need to be made of feminists materials. Feminist theory is world making.' (Sara Ahmed (2017) Living a Feminist Life, p. 14)

Basia Slivinska
Senior Lecturer in Cultural and Historical Studies,
University of the Arts, London

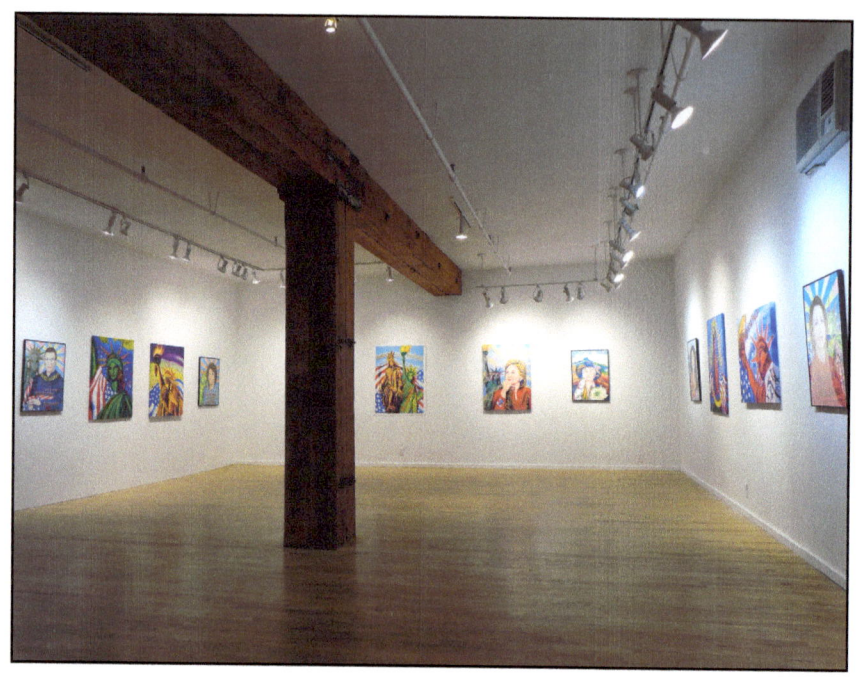

From Myth to Reality installation gallery One photo Kyra Belán

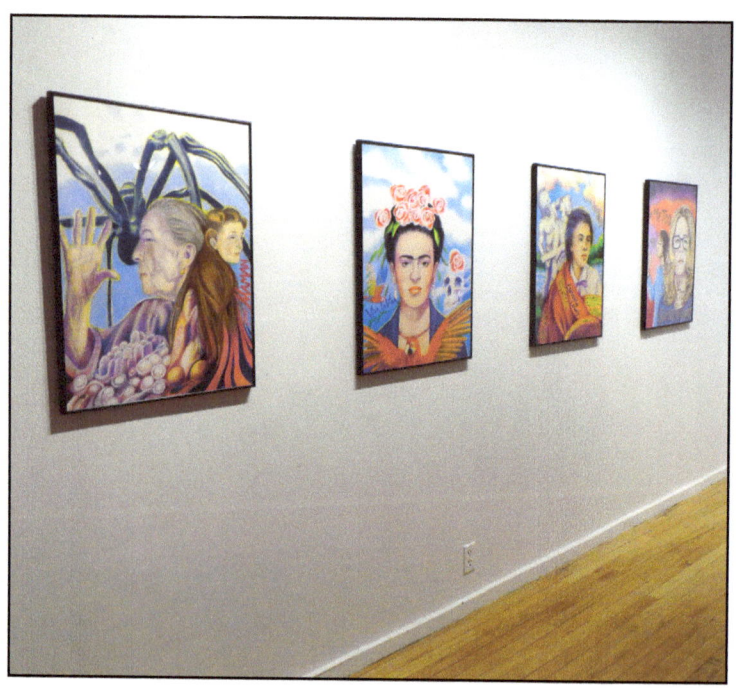

From Myth to Reality det. installation photo Kyra Belán

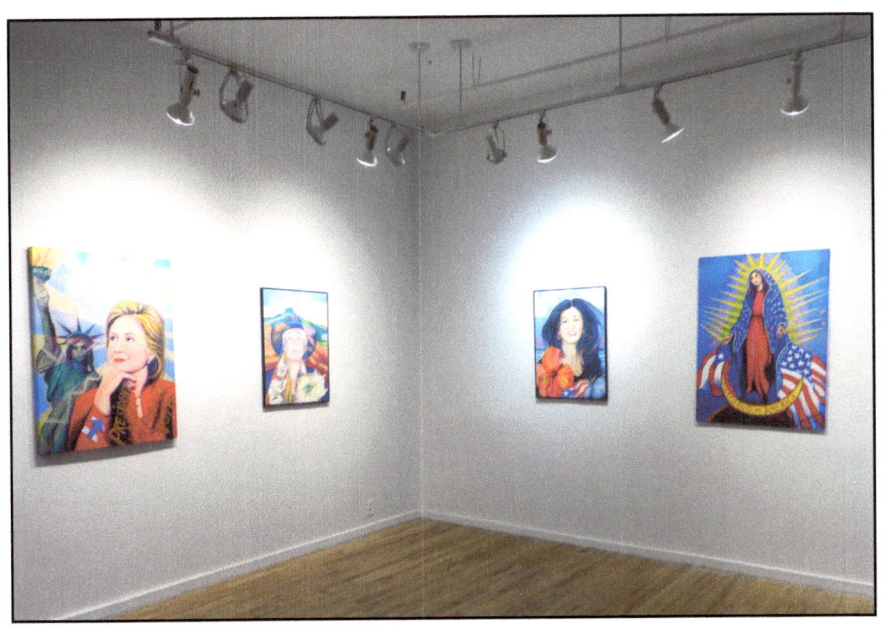

From Myth to Reality installation gallery One photo Kyra Belán

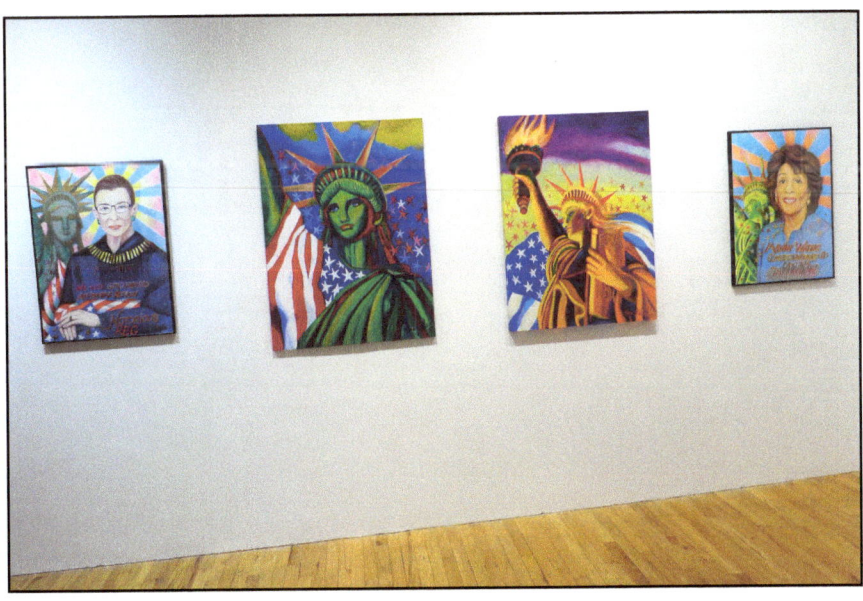

From Myth to Reality det. installation gallery One photo Kyra Belán

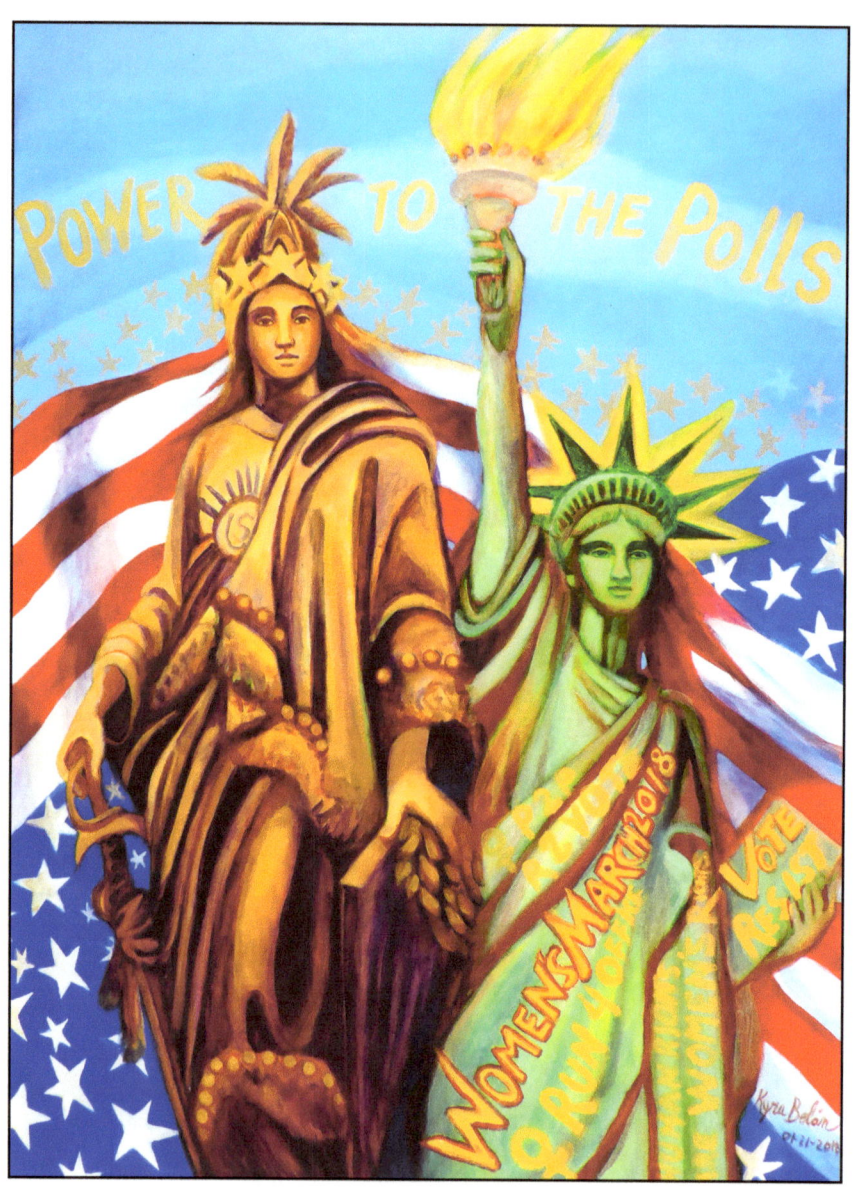

2018 WorldWide Women's March
acrylic painting on canvas 2018
48" x 36"

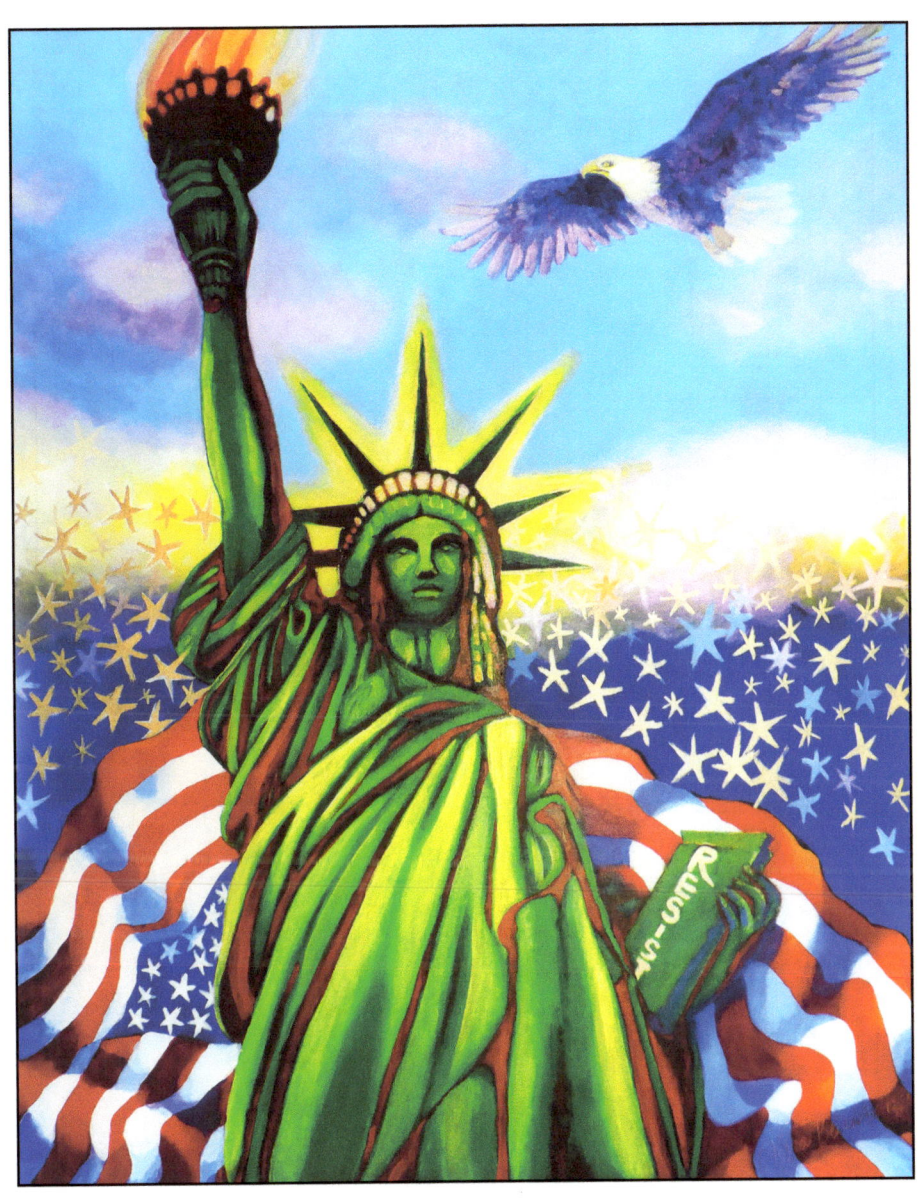

Resist
acrylic painting on canvas 2018
60" x 48"

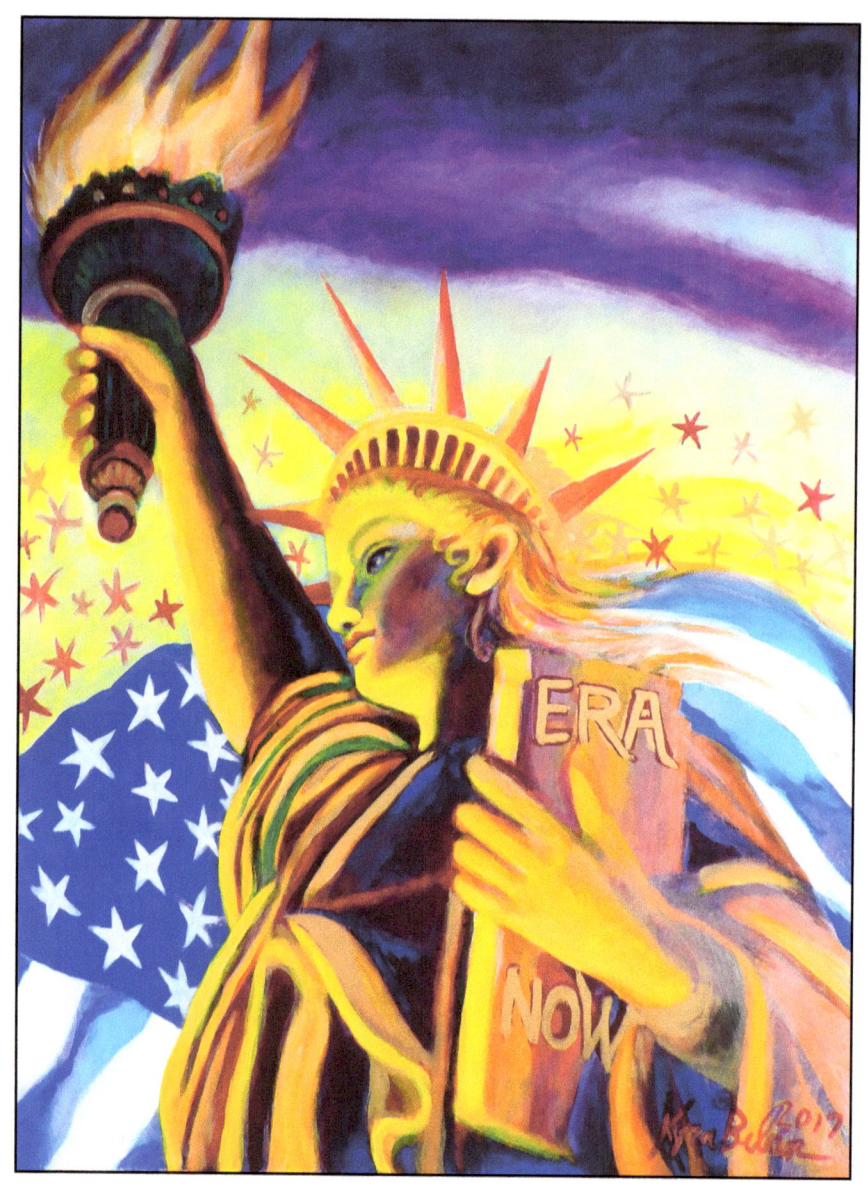

E.R.A. Now
acrylic painting on canvas 2017
40" x 30"

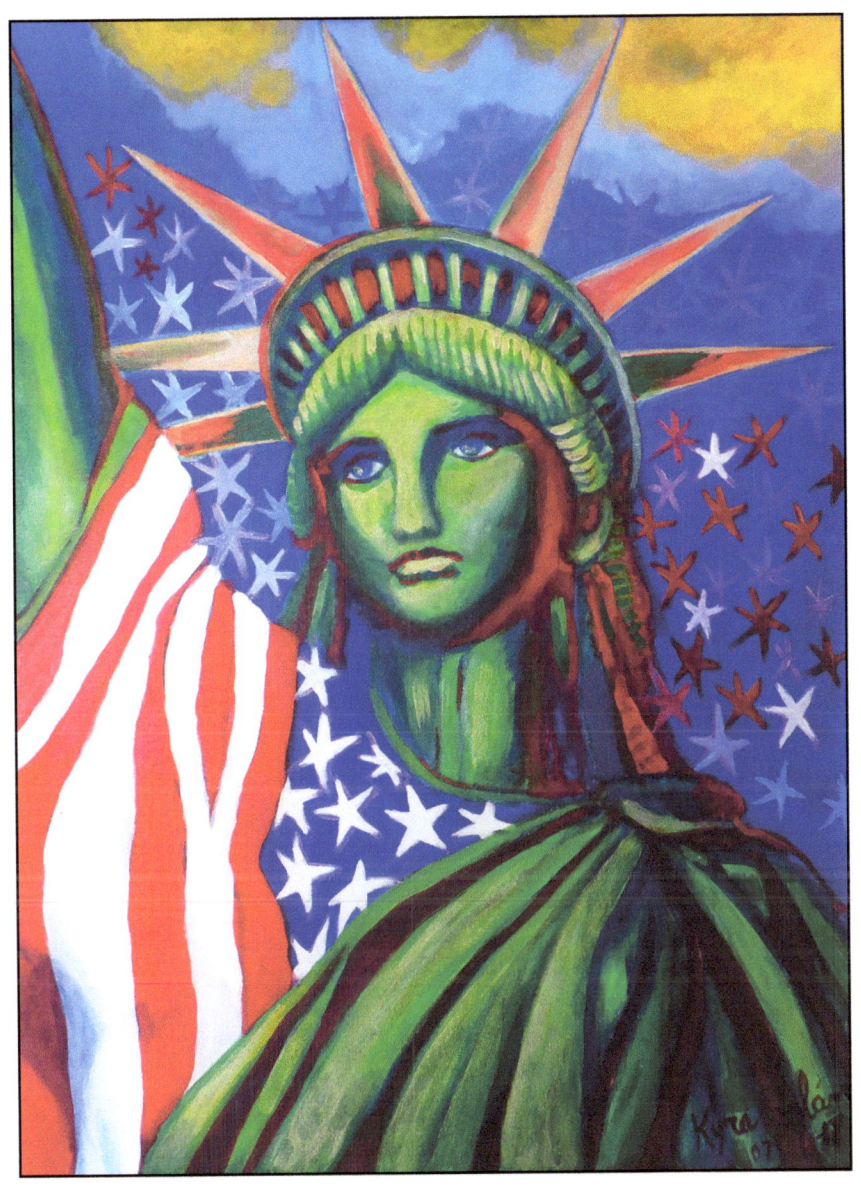

Demand Democracy
acrylic painting on canvas 2017
40" x 30"

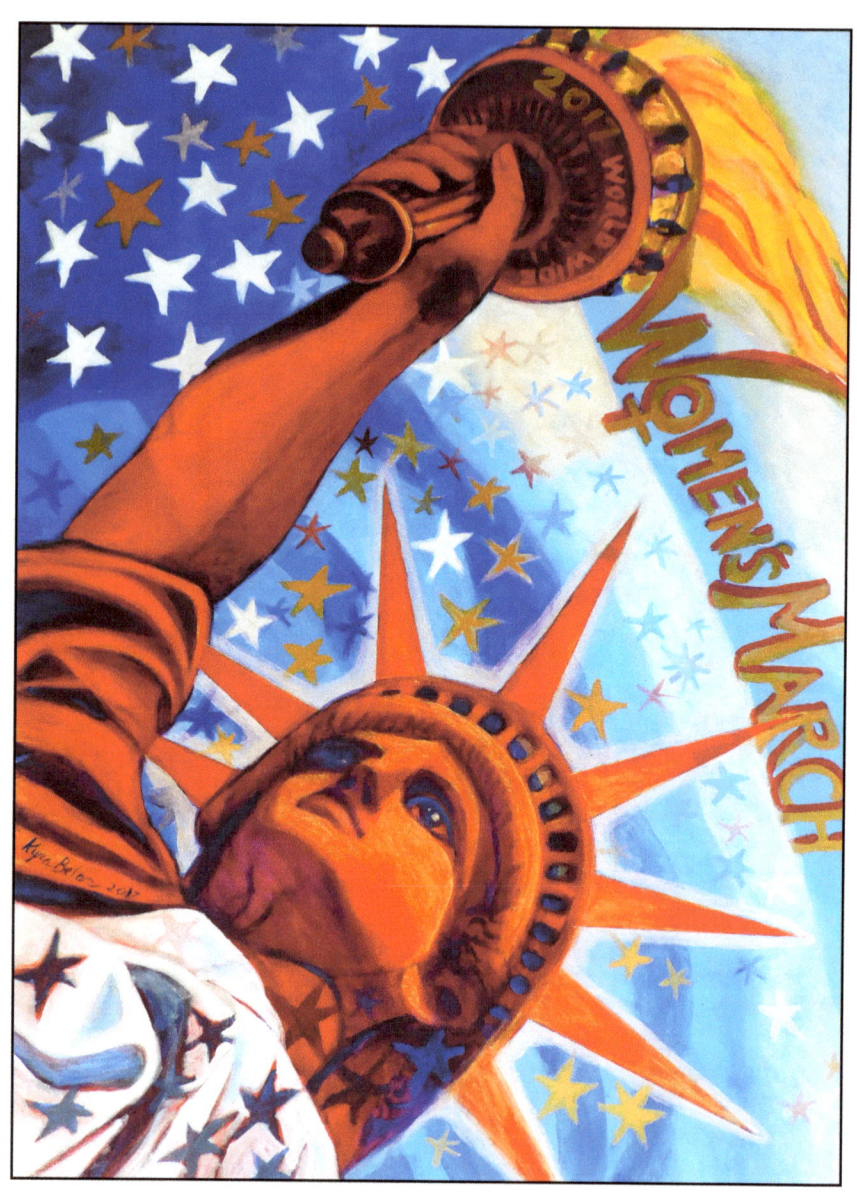

2017 WorldWide Women's March
acrylic painting on canvas 2017
40" x 30"

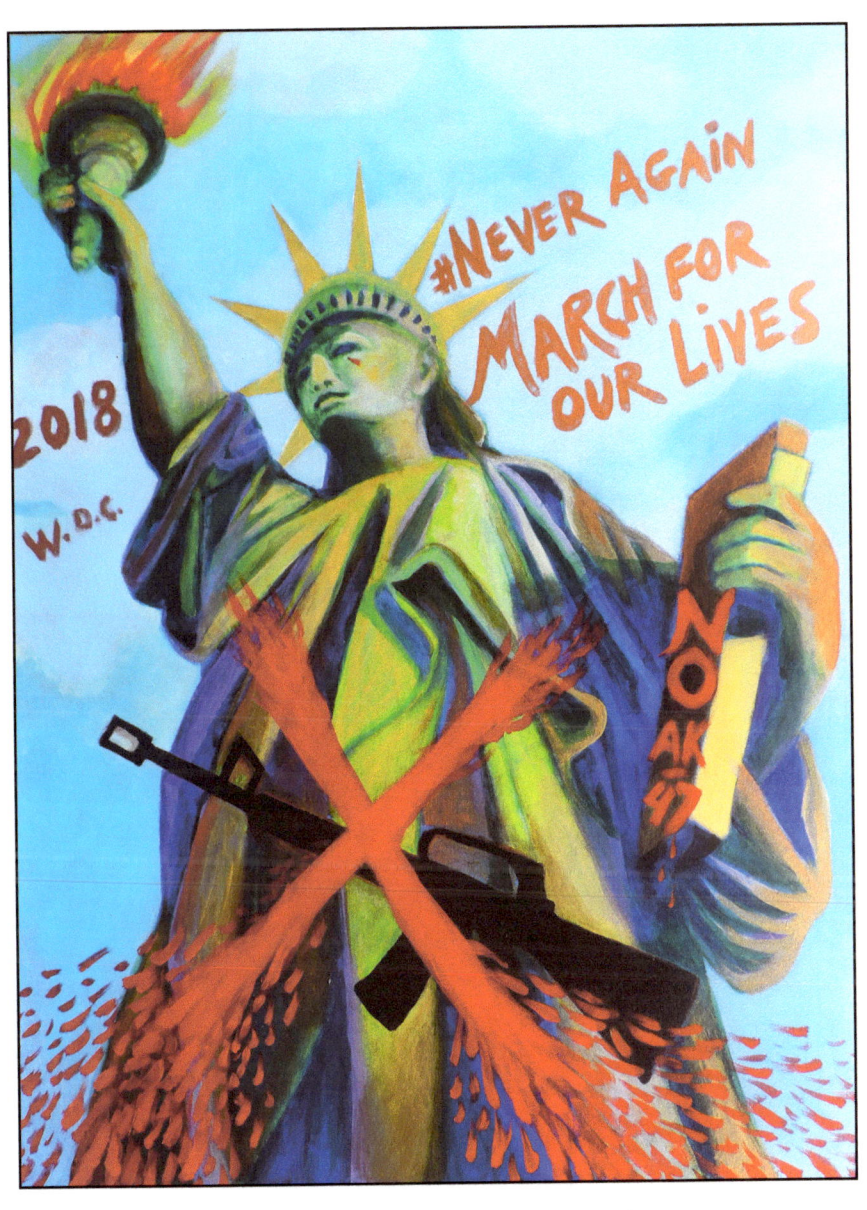

#Never Again March for our Lives
acrylic painting on canvas 2017
40" x 30"

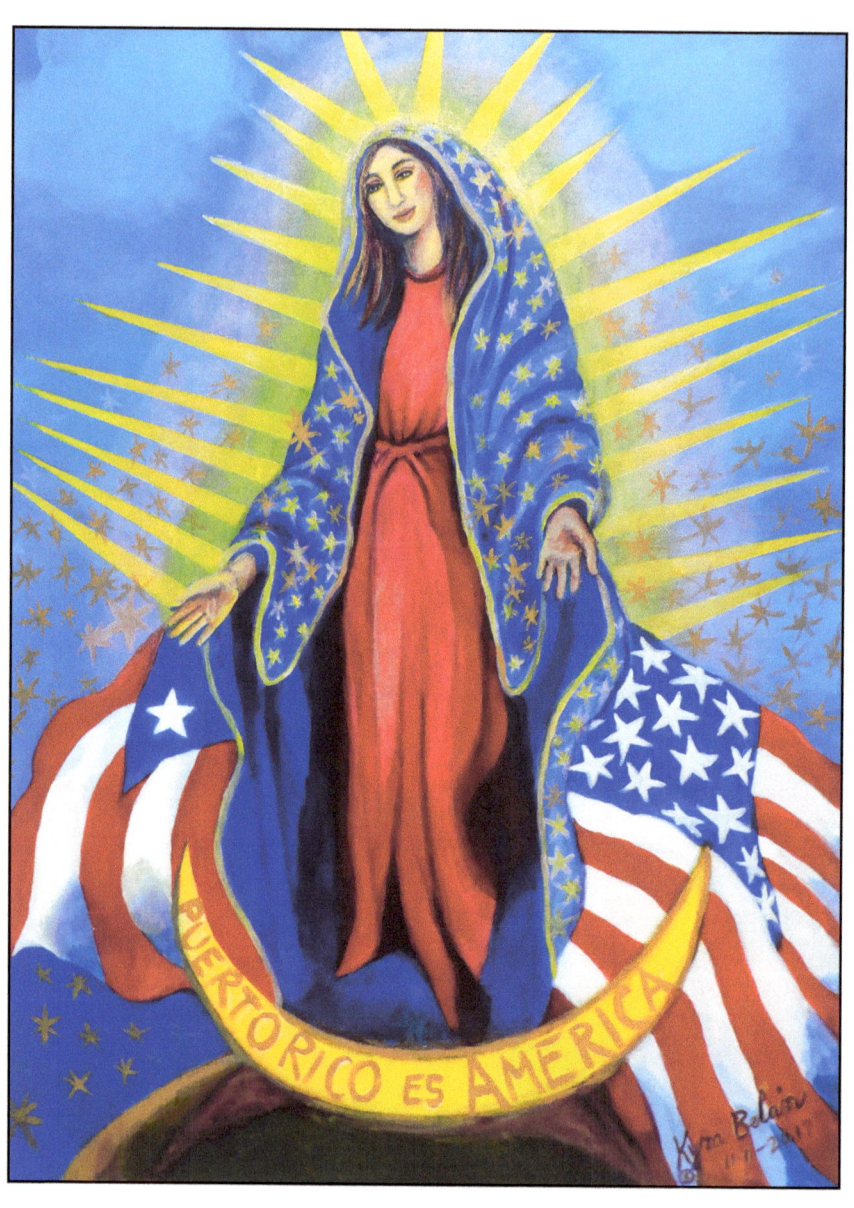

Puerto Rico Es America
acrylic painting on canvas 2017
40" x 30"

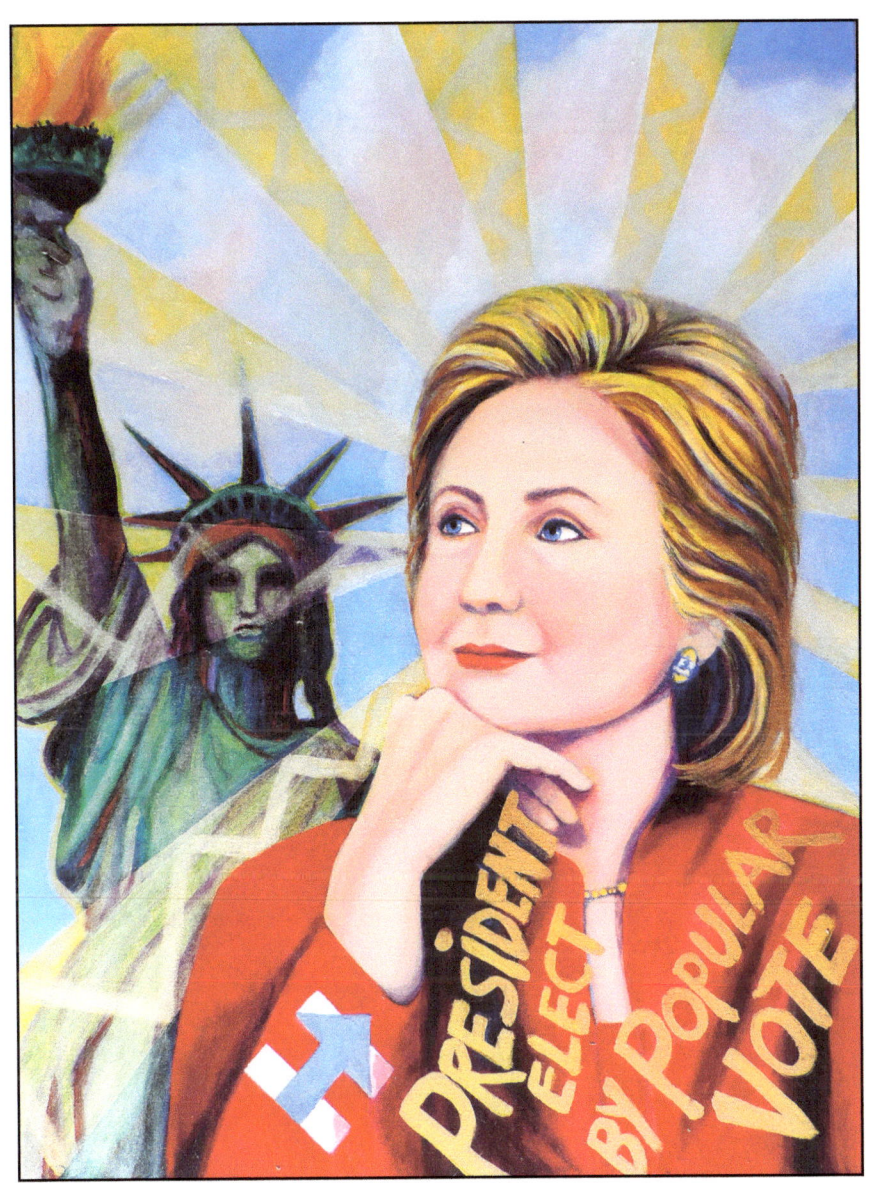

A Woman's Place is in the White House
acrylic painting on canvas 2016
40" x 30"

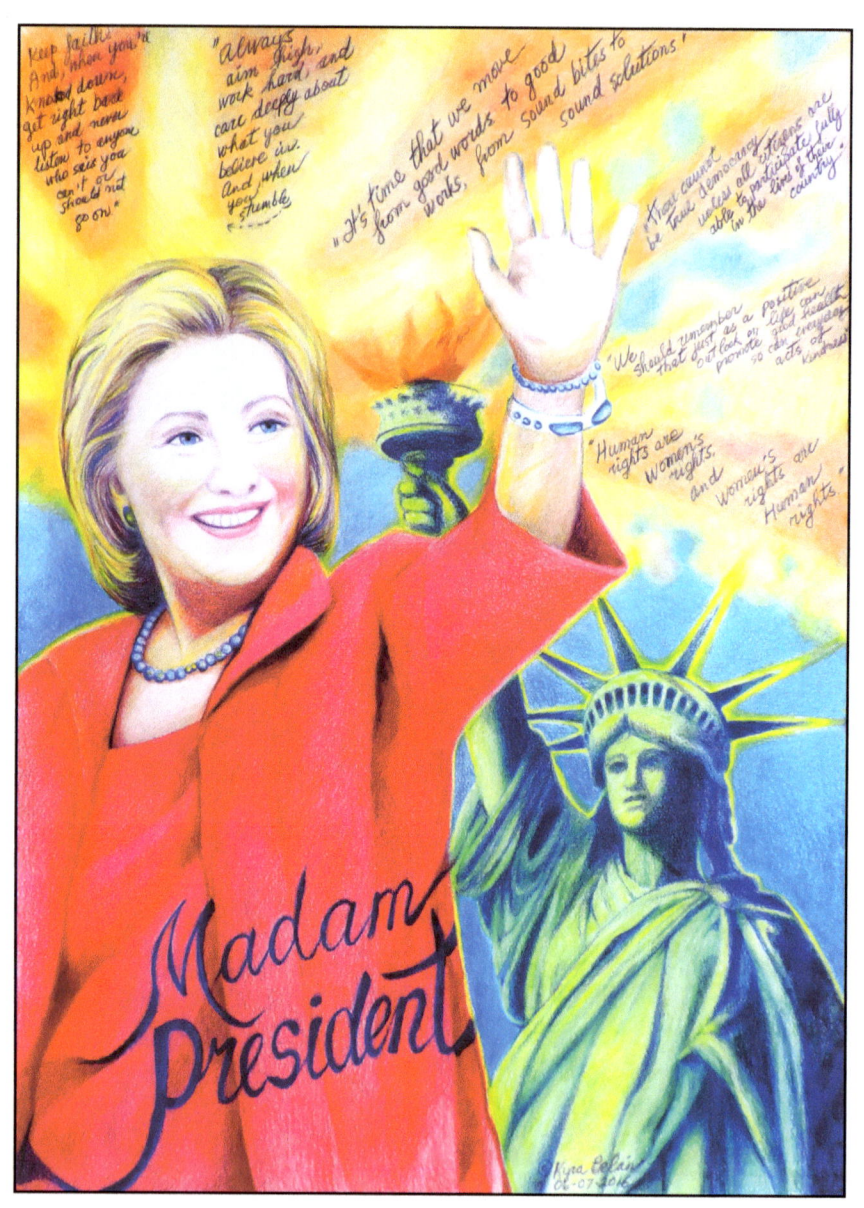

Madam President
colored pencil on paper 2016
(30" x 22")

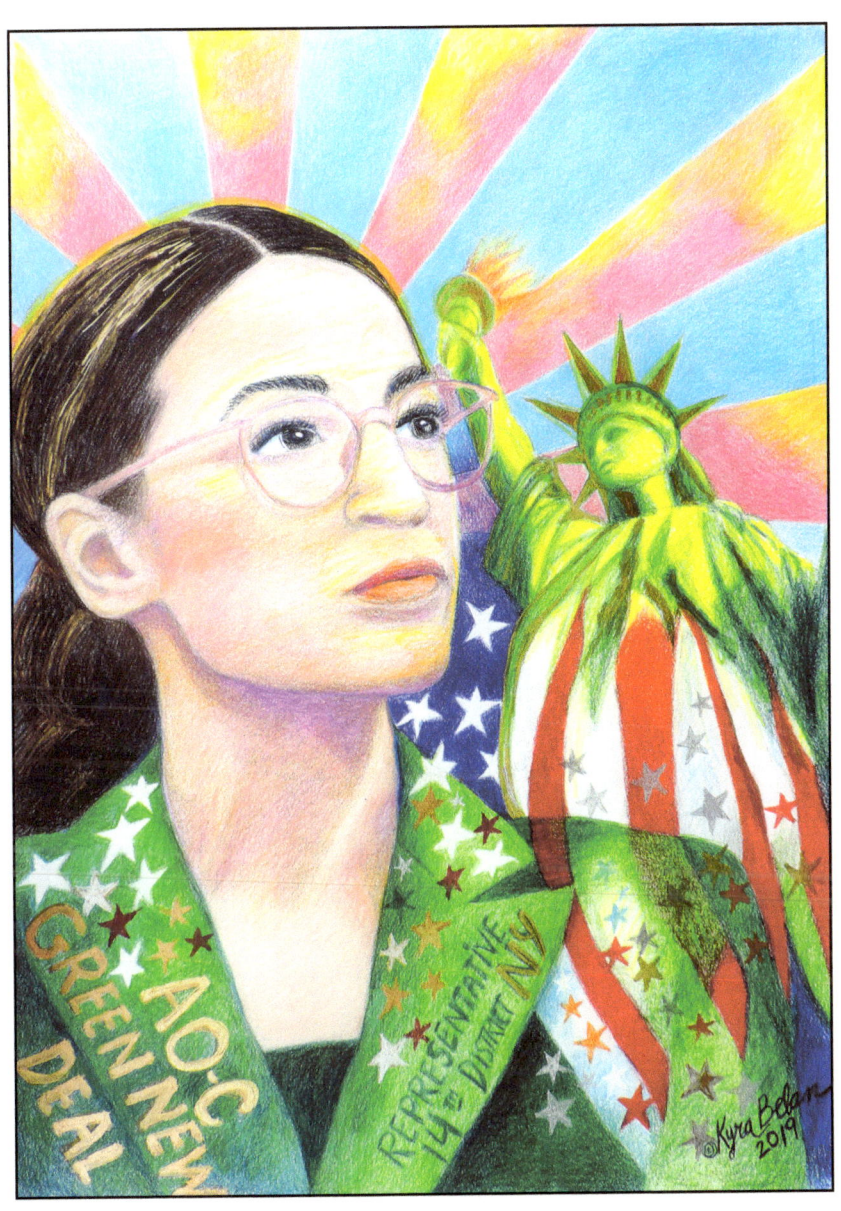

AO-C Green New Deal
colored pencil on paper 2019
(30" x 22")

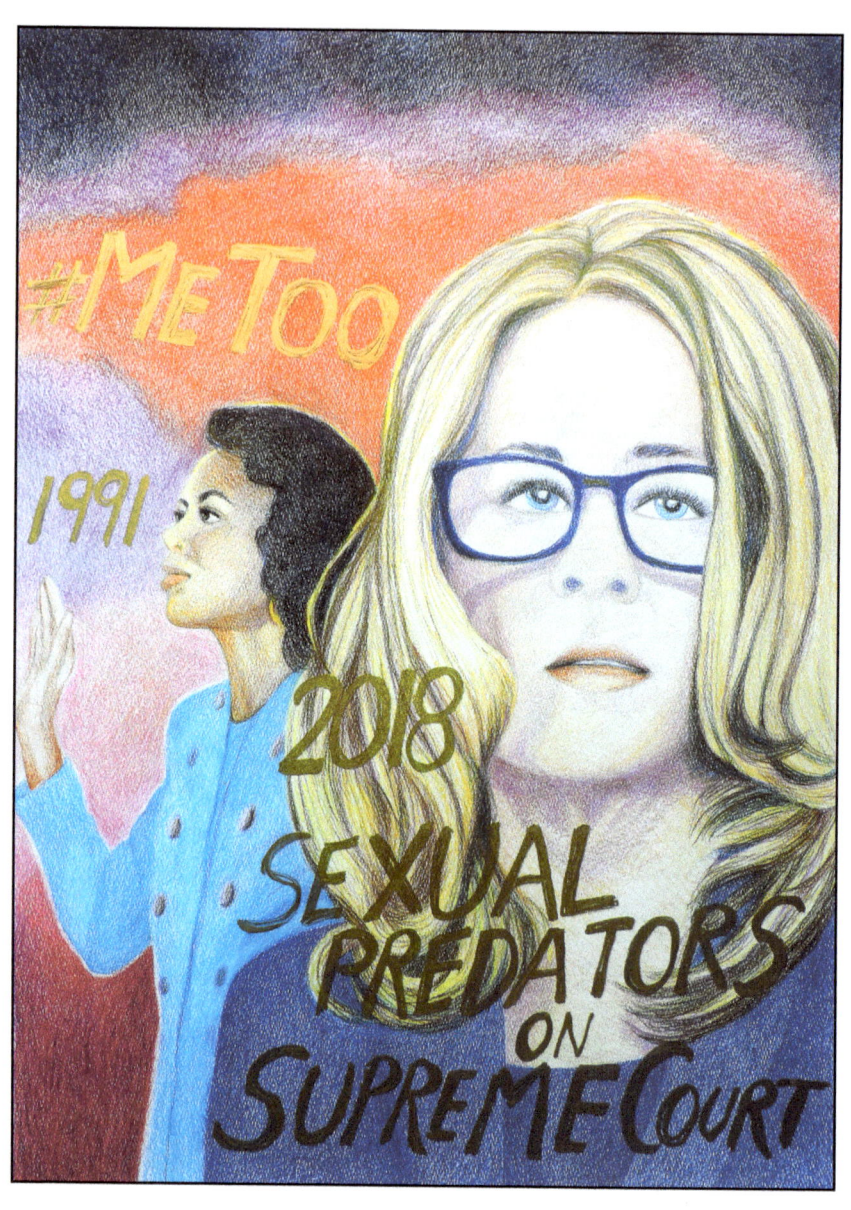

#Me TOO
colored pencil on paper 2018
(30" x 22")

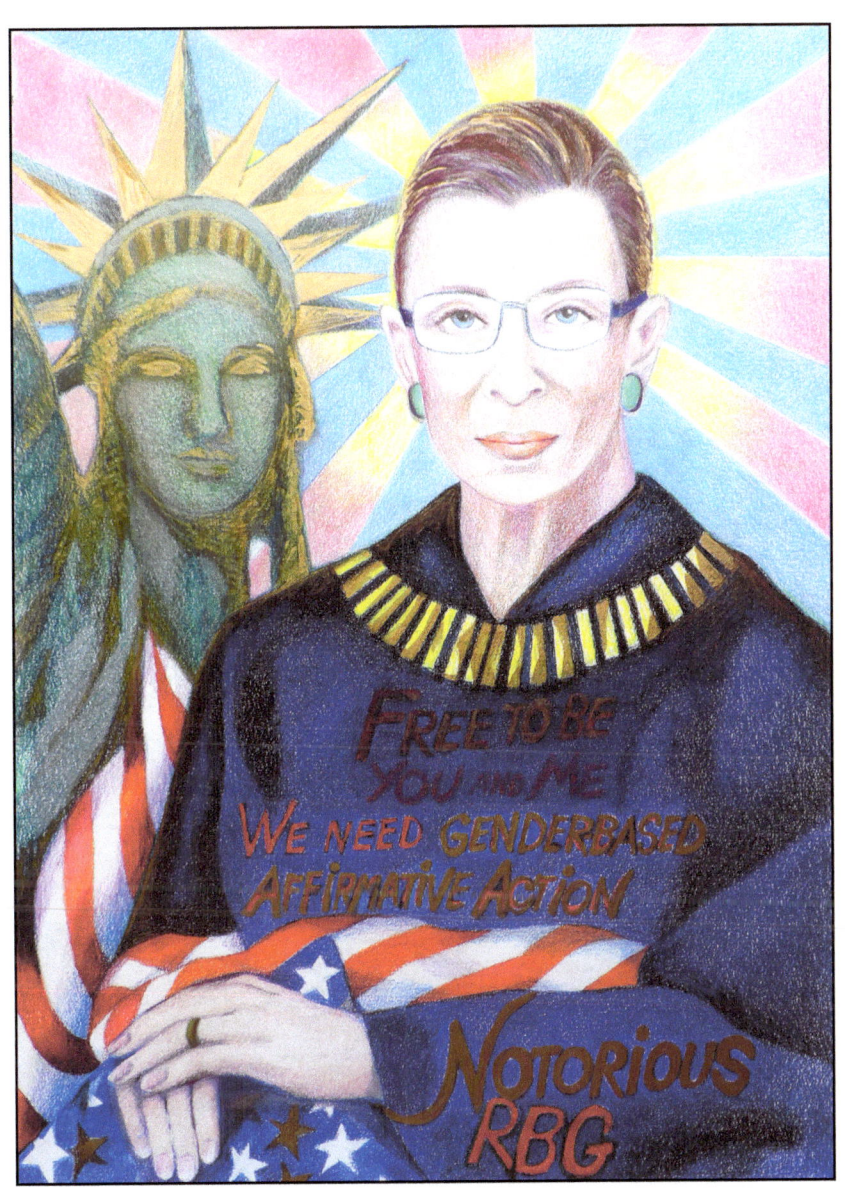

Notorious RBG
colored pencil on paper 2018
(30" x 22")

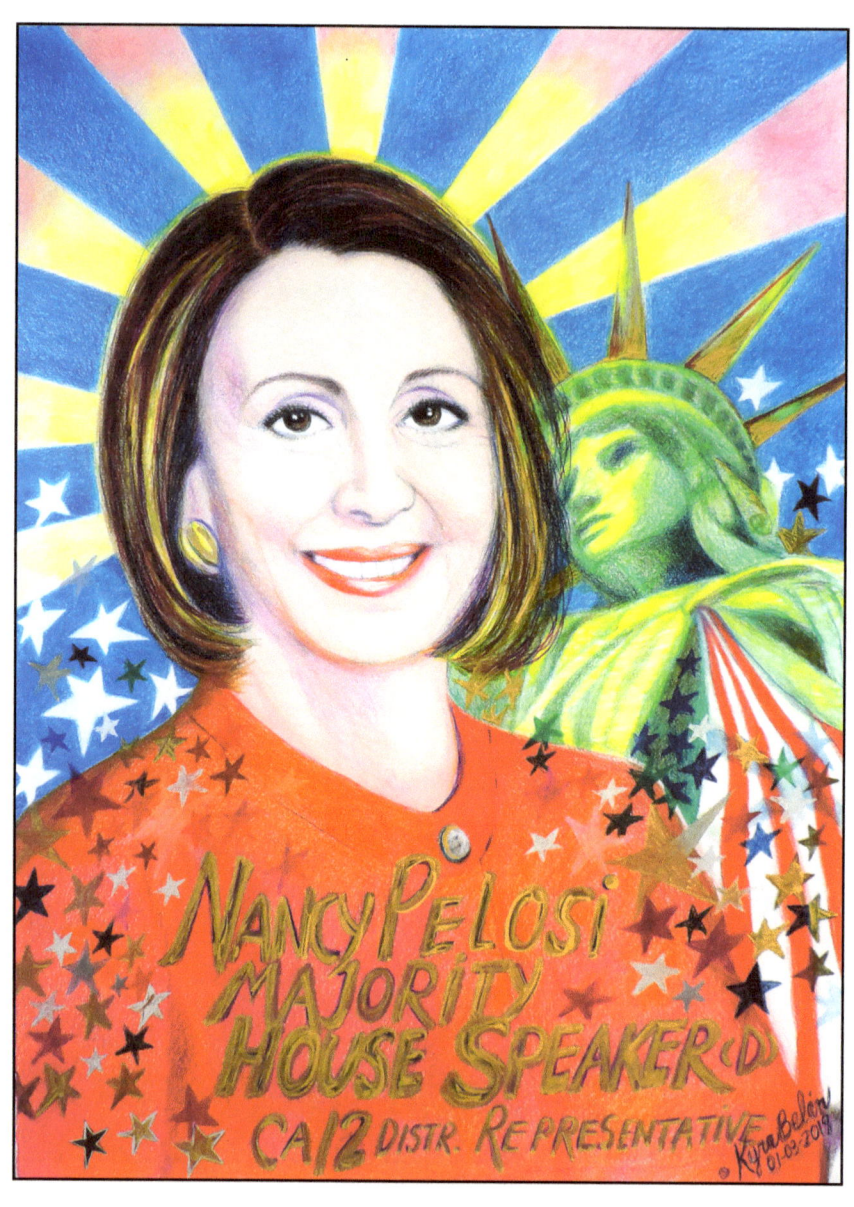

Nancy Pelosi
colored pencil on paper 2018
(30" x 22")

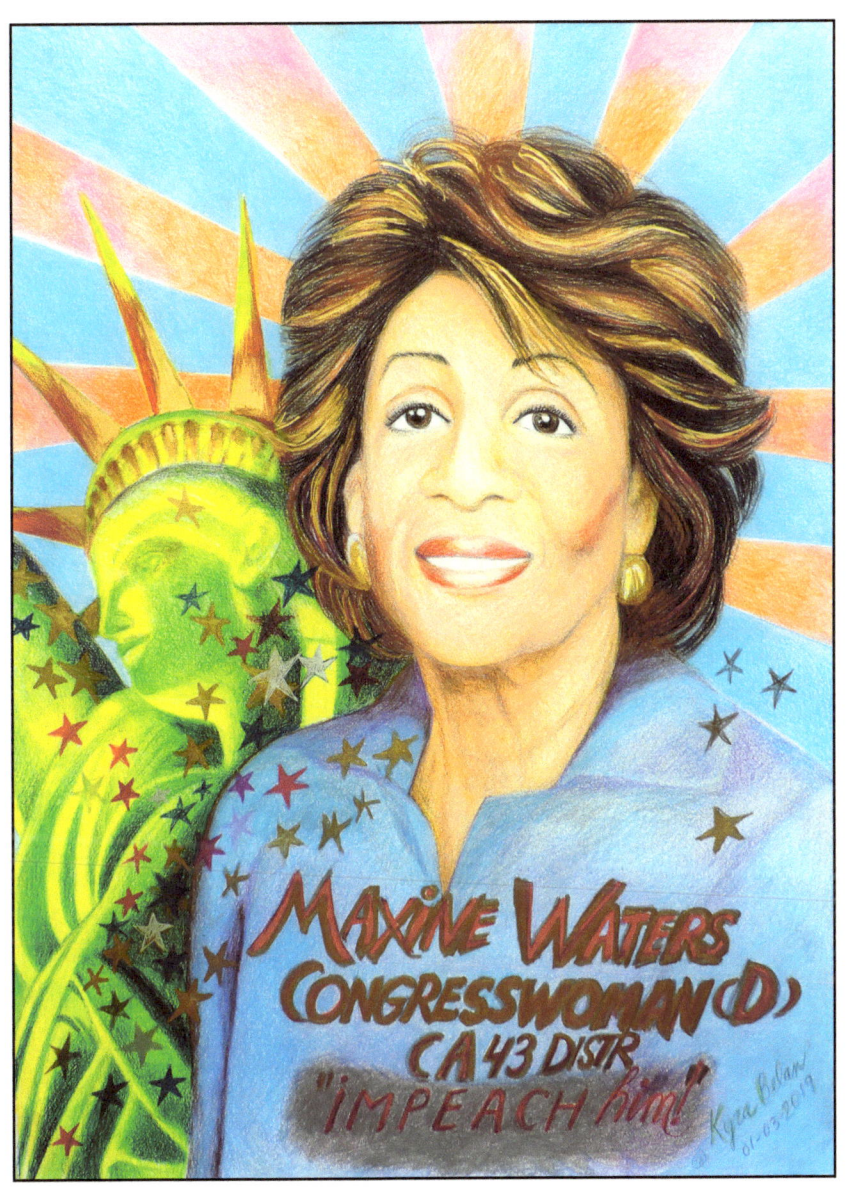

Maxine Waters
colored pencil on paper 2018
(30" x 22")

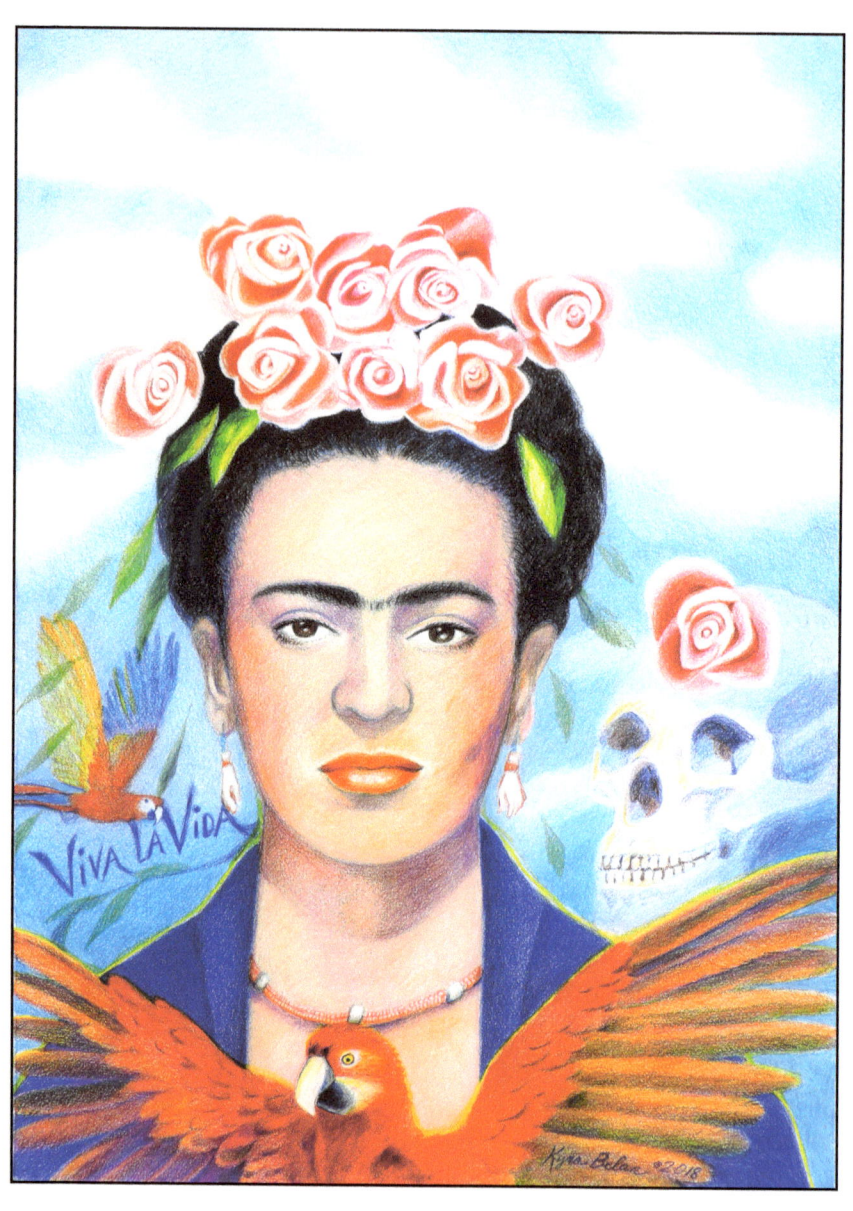

Frida Kahlo: Viva La Vida
colored pencil on paper 2018
(30" x 22")

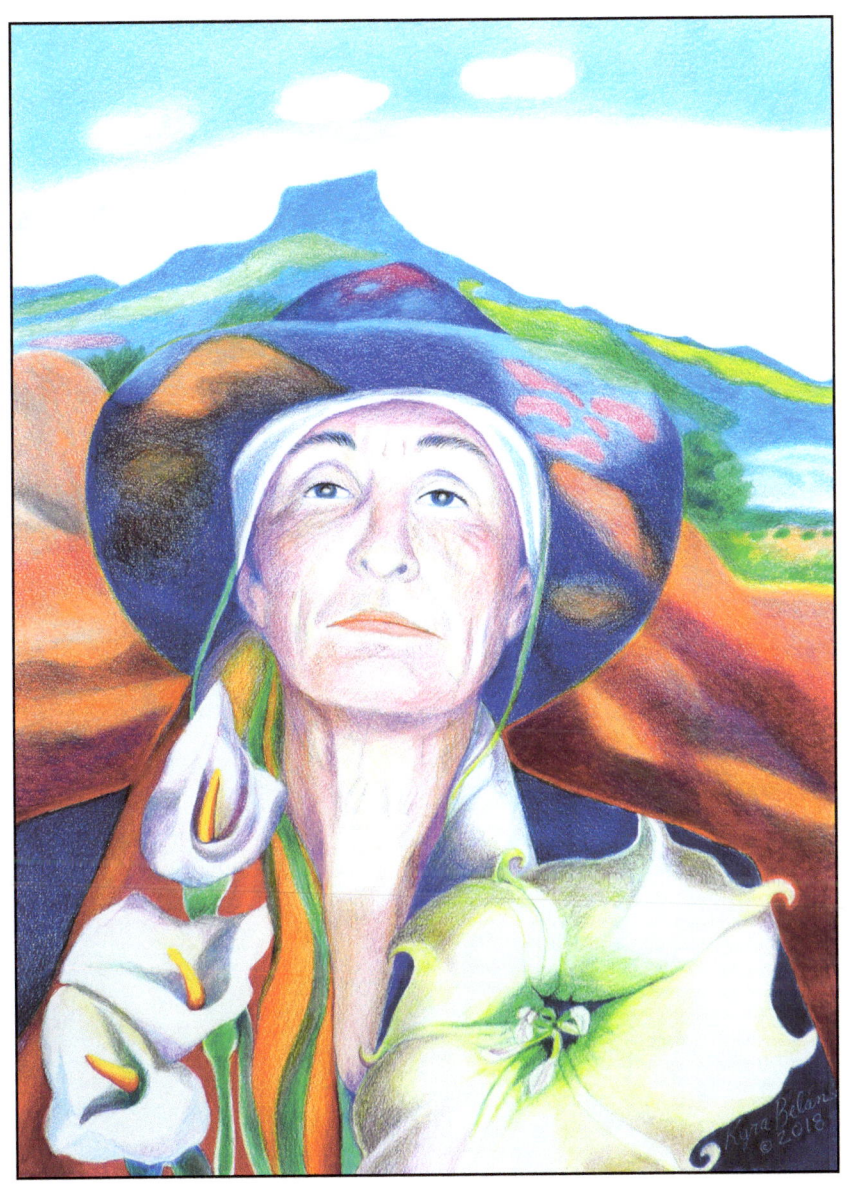

Georgia O' Keeffe with Jimson Weed and Cala Liles
colored pencil on paper 2018
(30" x 22")

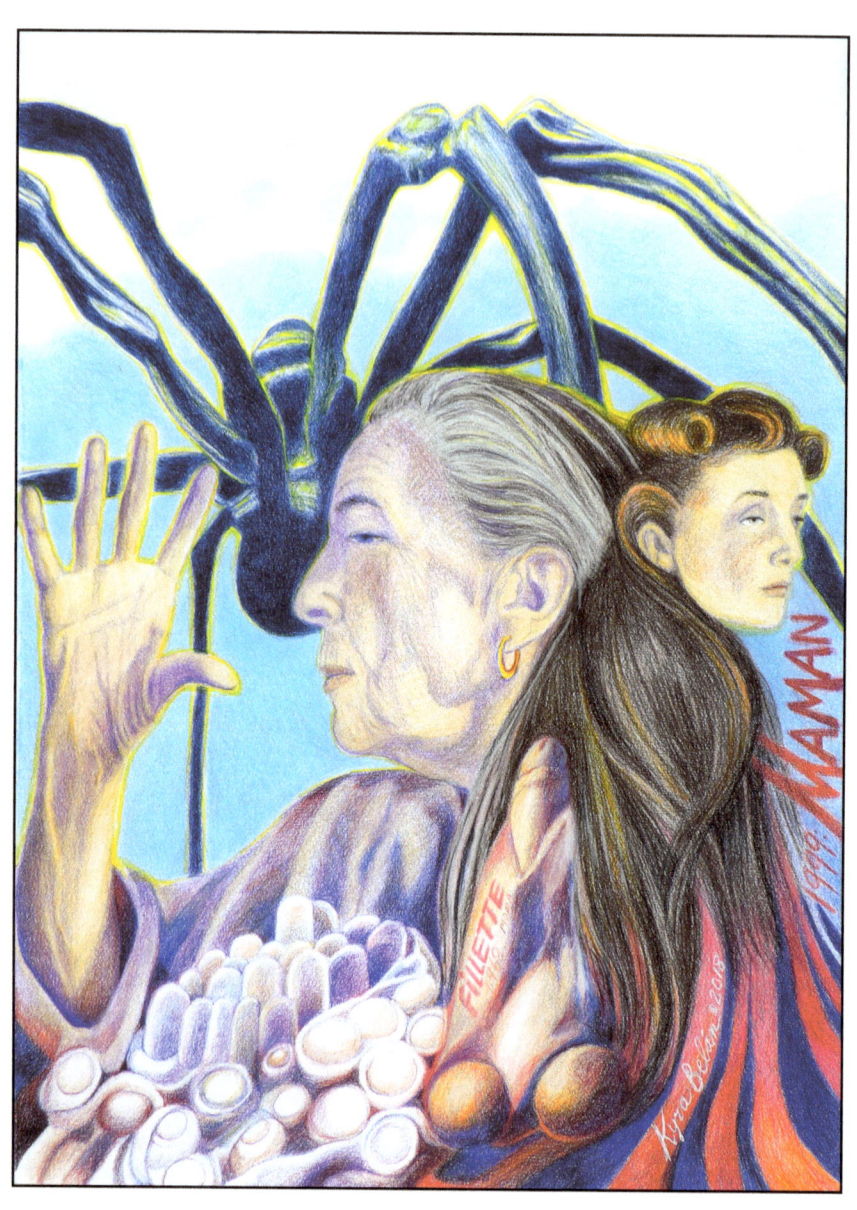

Louise Bourgeois: Maman
colored pencil on paper 2018
(30" x 22")

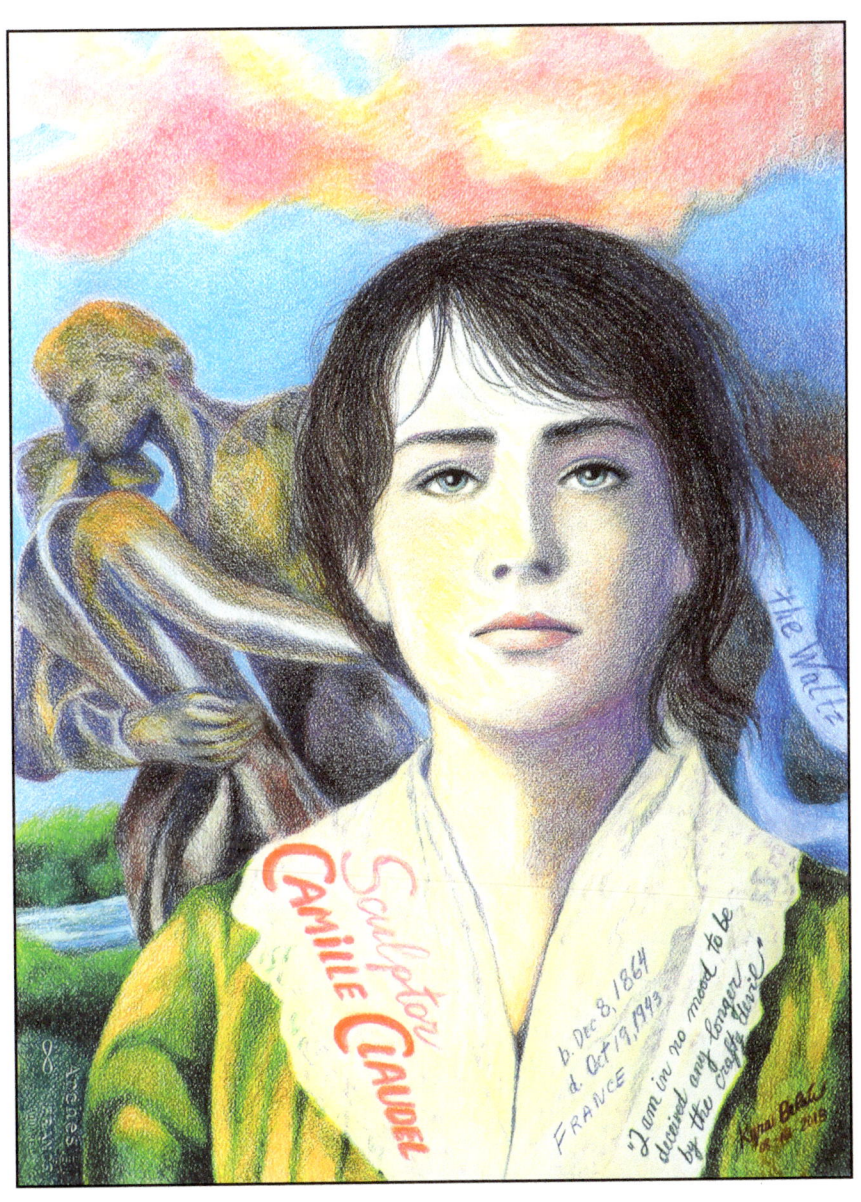

Camille Claudel: The Waltz
colored pencil on paper 2018
(30" x 22")

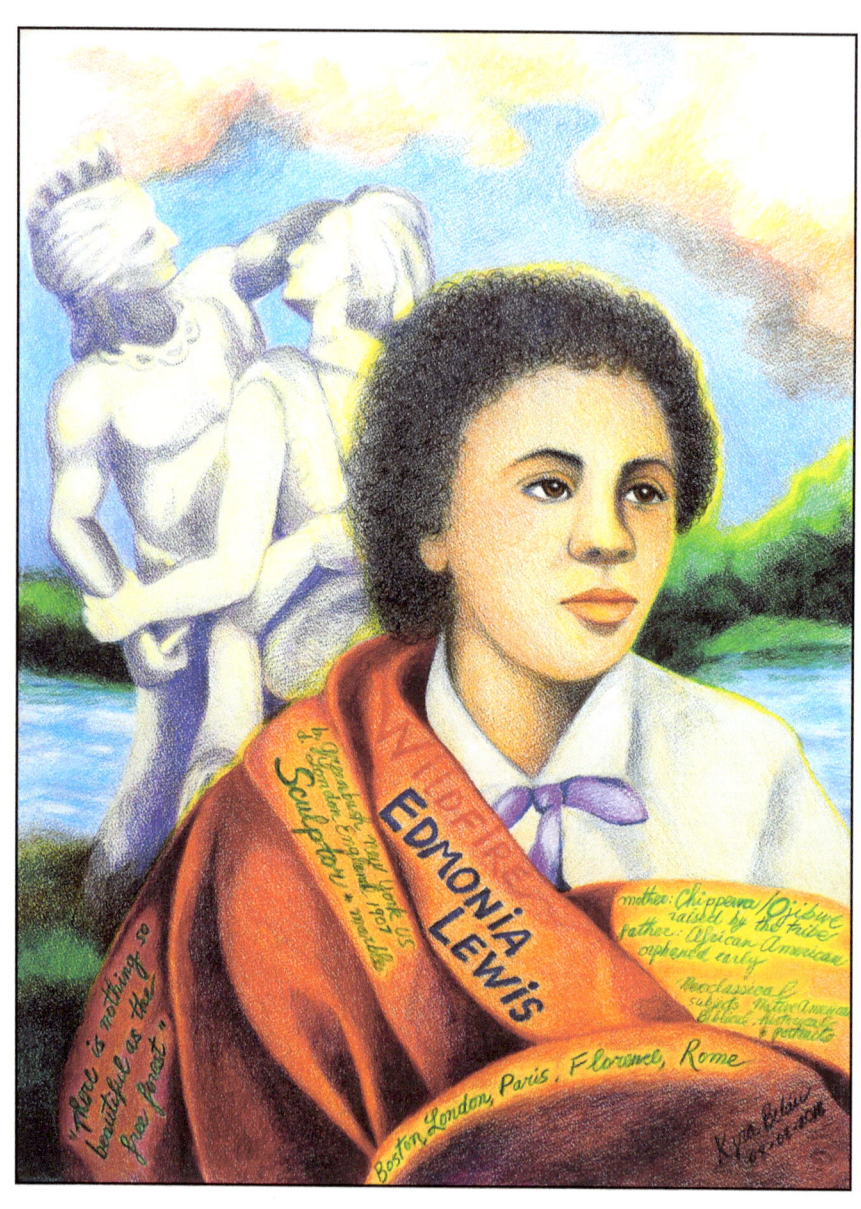

Wildfire Edmonia Lewis
colored pencil on paper 2018
(30" x 22")

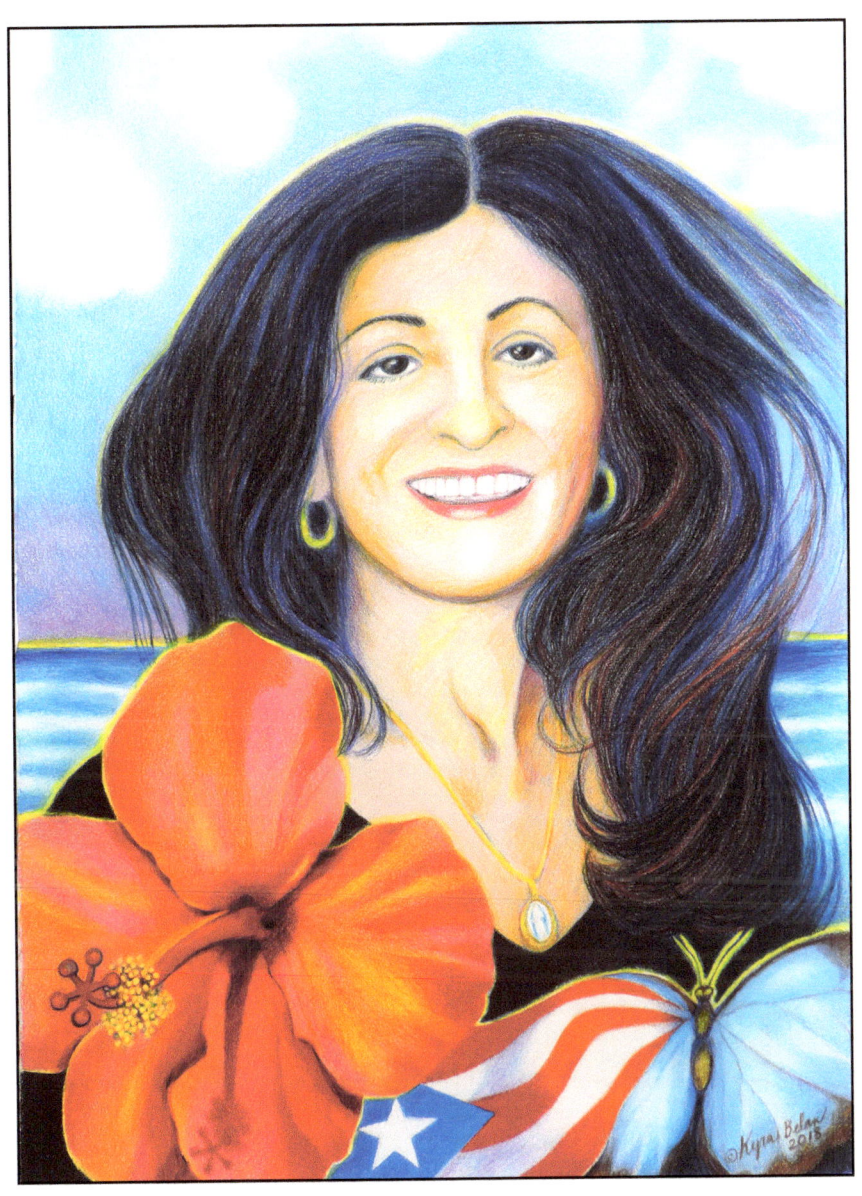

Judith Ortiz Cofer
colored pencil on paper 2018
(30" x 22")

Kyra Belán: From Myth to Reality

Ceres Gallery 547 W 27th St #201, New York, NY 10001
April 2 to April27 2019 Opening Thursday April 4 from 12-8 pm

List of Works

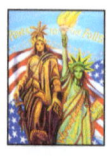

2018 WorldWide Women's March
Mixed media on canvas 2018
43" x 33"

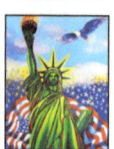

Resist
Mixed media on canvas 2018
43" x 33"

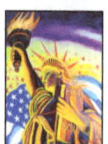

E.R.A. Now
acrylic painting on canvas 2017
40" x 30"

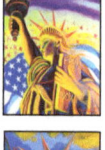

Demand Democracy
acrylic painting on canvas 2017
40" x 30"

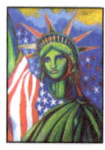

2017 WorldWide Women's March
acrylic painting on canvas 2017
40" x 30"

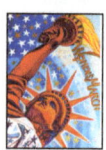

#Never Again March for our Lives
acrylic painting on canvas 2017
40" x 30"

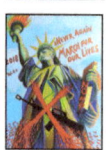

Puerto Rico Es America
acrylic painting on canvas 2017
40" x 30"

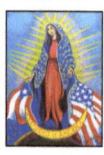

A Woman's Place is in the White House
acrylic painting on canvas 2016
40" x 30"

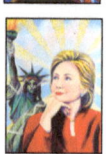

#Me TOO
colored pencil on paper 2018
30" x 22"

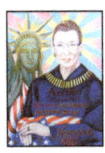
Notorious RBG
colored pencil on paper 2018
30" x 22"

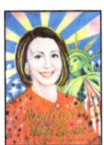
Nancy Pelosi
colored pencil on paper 2018
30" x 22"

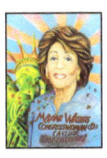
Maxine Waters
colored pencil on paper 2018
30" x 22"

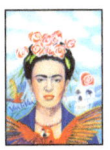
Frida Kahlo: Viva La Vida
colored pencil on paper 2018
30" x 22"

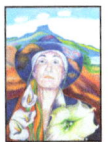
Georgia O' Keeffe with Jimson Weed
colored pencil on paper 2018
30" x 22"

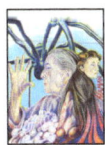
Louise Bourgeois: Maman
colored pencil on paper 2018
30" x 22"

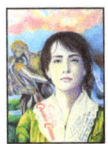
Camille Claudel: The Waltz
colored pencil on paper 2018
30" x 22"

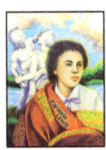
Wildfire Edmonia Lewis
colored pencil on paper 2018
30" x 22"

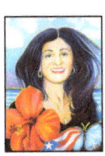
Judith Ortiz Cofer
colored pencil on paper 2018
30" x 22"

Dr. Kyra Belán

Otto M. Burkhardt Endowed Chair,
emerita professor of **art and art history**
and **gallery director, Broward College**

Website:http://www.kyrabelan.com
e-mail: kyrabelan2013@gmail.com
Cell: 954-829-2788
US citizen, origin: Argentina, b. China

Gallery Representation:
CERES Gallery, New York, NY
Artist Equity Gallery, New York, NY
Alliance for the Arts, Fort Myers, FL
Arts for ACT Gallery, Fort Myers. FL

EDUCATION:
Ed. D., Florida International University
M. F. A., Florida State University
B. F. A., Arizona State University

ARTIST/AUTHOR
PAINTING, DRAWING, MIXED MEDIA, PHOTOGRAPHY,
DIGITAL ART, INSTALLATION, LAND ART, PERFORMANCE ART

BOOKS:
THE VIRGIN AND CHILD
(Parkstone Press, translated to French and German) 2018
DIVINE LADIES IN AMERICA, Astarte Books, 2016
EARTH, MYTHS, AND ECOFEMINIST ART,
Createspace Independent Publishing, 2015
ART, MYTHS, AND RITUALS, BENT TREE PRESS, 2007
LA VIRGEN EN EL ARTE, PANAMERICANA PRESS, 2007
THE VIRGIN IN ART: FROM MEDIEVAL TO MODERN,
BARNES & NOBLE PRESS, 2005
EARTH, SPIRIT AND GENDER:
VISUAL LANGUAGE FOR THE NEW REALITY,
Forbes, '96,'98; Thomson, '01, '03; Benttree, 2005- 2010.
MADONNAS: From Medieval to Modern,
Parkstone Press '01, translated to French and German
Fiction: LUCID FUTURE: A SPIRITUAL ADVENTURE, Aegina Press,
2000; second ed., Create Space, 2012
co-author: Dorothy Gillespie, Radford University Press, '98

SELECTED HONORS, AWARDS AND GRANTS

Special Merit Award, Animals Juried Competition, Light, Space,
and Time Gallery, April 2015
Special Merit Award, Botanicals Juried Competition, Light, Space,
and Time Gallery, Jupiter, FL July 2014
Special Merit Award, Botanicals Juried Competition, Light, Space
and Time Gallery, Jupiter, FL August 2013
Third Place, Arts for Act Multi-Themed Juried Exhibition,
Ft Myers, Fl, July 2012
The Marquis Who's Who in American Art, '08,'09, '10, '11, 12.
13, 14, 15. 16
Florida Achievement Award in the Arts, Women's Caucus for Art
Florida Chapter, 2007-8
Cambridge Who's Who Registry of Executives and Professionals
07-08 vip member
Cambridge Who's Who Registry of Executives and Professionals 06-07
Honorable Mention, Summer International Exhibition, Museum of the
Americas, 2006
Southeastern Art Conference Award for Outstanding Artistic Achievement,
2005, U. of Arkansas at Little Rock
Annual ArtServe Encore Awards nominee 2002
Who's Who in American Art, 24th edition, 2001-2003
Otto M. Burkhardt Endowed Teaching Chair Recipient, BC, 1999-2002
Broward County Women's Hall of Fame Outstanding Achievement in the
Arts, FL,1999
Who's Who in American Art, 23rd edition, 1999-2000
International Woman of the Year, 1997/98, Cambridge, England
Who's Who in American Art, 22nd Edition, 1997-98
Who's Who in American Art, 21st Edition, 1995-96
Broward County Women's Hall of Fame Outstanding Achievement in the
Arts, nomination, 1994
Who's Who in American Art, 20th Edition, 1993-94
Who's Who in American Art, 19th Edition, 1992
Merit Award, Oswego International Video Festival, Oswego Art Center,
Oswego, NY, 1988
Who's Who of American Women, 15th edition, 1987/88
Who's Who in American Art, 17th edition, 1986
Merit Award. Expressions! The 6th Annual Competition And Exhibition,
Art and Culture Center of Hollywood, 1986/87
Money for Women - Barbara Deming Memorial Fund Grant, for the
Magic Circle Goddess Series, 1986
Metro-Dade Art in Public Places Commission, Miami, FL, 1986
Who's Who in the South and Southwest, 1985/86
Who's Who in America, 1985

Who's Who in the South and Southwest, 1984/85
Second Place, Graphics, Hollywood Creates 1983, Art and Culture Center of Hollywood, Hollywood, FL, 1983
Individual Artist Fellowship, State of Florida, Florida Fine Arts Council, 1982
Cover Art of special edition of The Miami Herald, Hooked on Hollywood, Greater Hollywood Chamber of Commerce, Hollywood, 1982
First Nationwide Savings Award, WPBT Channel 2 TV Juried Exhibition, Miami, FL, 1982
Mayor David Keating Award, Greater Hollywood Creates 1981, Art and Culture Center of Hollywood, Hollywood, FL, 1981
Gene Segal Award, WPBT Channel 2 TV Juried Exhibition, Metropolitan Museum and Art Center, Coral Gables, FL, 1981
Broward Art in Public Places, Commission for Southern Regional Courthouse, Hollywood, FL, 1981
Limited Edition Award, WPBT Channel 2 TV, Miami, FL, 1980

SELECTED ART IN PUBLIC COLLECTIONS
Art and Culture Center, Hollywood, FL
ArtServe, Ft. Lauderdale, FL
Bass Museum of Art, Miami Beach, FL
Broward Art in Public Places, South Regional Courthouse, Hollywood, FL
Broward College, Pembroke Pines, FL
Lake Eustis Museum of Art: LEMA, Eustis, FL
Meadows School of the Arts, Southern Methodist University, Dallas, TX.
Museum of the Americas, Doral, FL
Museum of Fine Arts, Florida State University, Tallahassee, FL
Metro-Dade Art in Public Places, Miami, FL
Orange County Arts & Cultural Affairs Art Collection, Orlando, FL
University of Central Florida, School of Performing Arts, Orlando, FL
Sidney and Berne Davis Art Center, Fort Myers, FL
Edison and Ford Winter Estates, Fort Myers, FL

AND NUMEROUS PRIVATE COLLECTIONS

SELECTED ONE ARTIST EXHIBITIONS:
Kyra Belan, Resist, CAA Artspace, Los Angeles Convention Center CAA Annual Conference, February 2018
Kyra Belan Symbolic Magic: Installation, SBDAC Fort Myers, FL April 2017
Kyra Belan Solo Exhibition, Spectrum Miami 2016, December 2016
Kyra Belan: Magical Paradise, Broadway Palm Fine Art Gallery, April-May 2016
Kyra Belan, Installation: Rosa Sinensis, Arts for ACT main Gallery, November 2015

Kyra Belan: Recent Artworks, Cape Coral City Hall Art Gallery,
November-December 2014

Kyra Belan: Paintings, Digital Mixed Media, Cape Coral Library
Art Gallery, September – October 2014

Kyra Belan: American Beauty Series, Broadway Palm Art Gallery,
Fort Myers, FL May 26 – June 22, 2014

Kyra Belan: Paintings, Drawings, Mixed, Digital, The Alliance for
the Arts, Fort Myers FL December 2013

Kyra Belan: Installation: American Beauty, Fine Arts Gallery, Cape Coral
Arts Studio, Cape Coral, FL Dec. 2013

Kyra Belan: Sacred Ladies, Arts for ACT Gallery, Fort Myers, FL
September, 2013

Four Artists, Visual Arts Center, Punta Gorda, FL January 2013

American Beauty Series: Paintings, Guest Artist exhibition, Harbor View
Gallery, Cape Coral, FL August 2012

Art, Myths, and Rituals: Paintings and digital art, Arts for Act,
Fort Myers, FL February 2012

Mother Earth, Thought Woman: Mixed Media Installation, The Art
Gallery, BC South, Jan-Feb 2009

Lady Liberty and Other Archetypes, digital art installation and ritual
performance; Magic Circle XXIX, The Art Gallery, BC South,
March-April 2004

Spirit Circle, digital art; installation and ritual performance:
Magic Circle XXVIII, The Art Gallery, BC South, 1999-2000

Celebration of Mother Earth: Magic Circle XXVII, earth art
and ritual performance, Rochester
Institute of Technology, Rochester, NY. 1998

Goddess of the World: Magic Circle XXVI, site specific installation and
ritual performance, The Art and Culture Center of Hollywood, FL.
1996-97

The Floralia Series, site specific installation of paintings, The Art and
Culture Center of Hollywood, FL. 1995

Goddess Lakshmi: Magic Circle XXV, site specific installation and
ritual solstice performance, Yoga Vedanta Science and Arts Center, Ft.
Lauderdale. FL. 1994

Mother Earth, Changing Woman: Magic Circle XXIV: site specific
installation and ritual performance, The Art Gallery, Broward College,
Pembroke Pines, FL, 1994

Mother Earth, Mother God: Magic Circle XXIII, site specific installation
and ritual performance, The 621 Gallery, Tallahassee, FL, 1993

Magic Circle XXII: Celebration for Goddess Juno, Sri Naranda Yoga
Centre, Hallandale, FL, 1993

Goddess Sulis: Magic Circle XXI, performance, Salisbury, England, 1992

Our Lady of Florida: Magic Circle XX, The Art Gallery, Broward College, Pembroke Pines, FL, 1991

Great Goddess Gaia - A Celebration: Magic Circle XIX, 15th Annual Holiday Festival, Broward Art Guild, Fort Lauderdale, FL, 1990

Great Goddess Chalchiutlicue: Magic Circle XVIII, The Rim Institute, Payson, AZ, 1989

Great Goddess Chicomecoatl/Shakti: Magic Circle XVII, The Rim Institute, Payson, AZ, 1988

Great Goddess Rhea: Magic Circle XVI, performance, Malia, Crete, Greece, 1988

Cosmic Goddess Chicomecoatl/Demeter: Magic Circle XV, Dupont Gallery, Washington and Lee University, Lexington, VA, 1988

Great Goddess Chicomecoatl: Magic Circle XIV, Art and Culture Center of Hollywood, Hollywood, FL, 1987

Great Goddess Medusa: Magic Circle XIII, Fine Arts Gallery, Broward College, Davie, FL, 1987

Nature Goddess Sekhmet: Magic Circle XII, Miami Site, Key Biscayne, FL, 1987

Sun Goddess, Emergence of Myth: Magic Circle XI, Fine Arts Gallery, Broward College, Davie, FL, 1986

The Magic Circle Series 1978 - 1985, Einstein Library, Nova University, Davie, FL, 1985

Great Goddess: Magic Circle X, Metropolitan Museum and Art Center, Coral Gables, FL, 1985

In Quest of the American Goddess Coatlicue: Magic Circle IX, Fine Arts Gallery, Broward College, Davie, FL ,1985

Great American Indian Goddess Coatlicue: Magic Circle VIII, Fine Arts Gallery, Broward College, Davie, FL, 1984

Goddess Isis: Magic Circle VII, New World Campus, Miami-Dade College, Miami, FL, 1984

Magic Birds of Florida, The Gallery, Bailey Hall, Broward College, Davie, FL, 1983

Goddess: Magic Circle VI, Fine Arts Gallery, Broward College, Davie, FL, 1982

Isis: Magic Circle V, Broward College, Pembroke Pines, FL,1982

Tropical Magic, Florida Atlantic University Library, Boca Raton, FL, 1981

Magic Florida, Art and Culture Center of Hollywood, Hollywood, FL, 1980

Goddess Isis: Magic Circle IV, Unitarian Church, Fort Lauderdale, FL, 1980

SELECTED JURIED, INVITATIONAL, FACULTY or ART FAIR EXHIBITIONS

Identity, members exhibition, Alliance for the Arts, Fort Myers, FL, August 17 – September 30, 2018

Artblend Art Gallery Invitational Exhibition, August – September 2018

Raising Women's Voices, Ceres Gallery, NY, May 22 - June 16, 2018
Market Art & Design Expo Hamptons NY 2018, Artblend Artist Agency,
NY 2018
Artblend Art Gallery Invitational Exhibition, Fort Lauderdale FL
May – June 2018
Art Expo New York 2018, Artblend Artist Agency, New York, 2018
Spectrum Miami 2017, Artblend Artist Agency, Miami, FL 2017
ADC Fine Art, Blink Art Juried Exhibition, Cincinnati, OH
June-July 2017
Now See Us Hear Us, Sediment Art Gallery, Richmond VA February 2017
Politico, juried exhibition, Alliance for the Arts, Fort Myers FL
September 2016
Founding Females Portrait Exhibition, Edison and Ford Winter Estates,
March 2016
International Print Festival in Italy, Arte in Centro, Bergamo, Italy,
June 2015
NLAPW SE Branch Exhibition, Sidney and Berne Art Center, Fort Myers,
FL March 2015
Basel-Christmas, International Art Exhibition, Museum of the Americas,
Doral, FL Dec 5 -2014 – Jan 2-2015
Juried Exhibition, org. by Museum of the America, Caroussel de Louvre,
Paris, France 2014
Art Takes Miami, SeeMe and Scope Art Fifth Annual, Booth G19,
1001 Ocean Dr, Miami Beach, FL Dec 2014
Diametrically Opposed Members Exhibition, Alliance for the Arts,
Fort Myers, FL August 8 – August 29, 2014
Elements of ARTchitecture, Sidney & Berne Davis Art Center, Fort Myers,
FL June 6 – June 26, 2014
II Premio Internacional Don Quijote de la Mancha, Crisolart Gallery,
Barcelona, Spain, group exhibition/catalog, March 28-April17, 2014
Women's Rights: An Artist's Perspective, UniteWomen.Org juried online
exhibition and catalog, 2013
Black and White Members Exhibit, Alliance for the Arts, Fort Myers, FL,
August – September 2012
Annual Arts for ACT Preview Exhibit, Bob Rauschenberg Gallery,
Edison College, Ft. Myers, FL July 13 – August 8, 2012
Summer Member Exhibit, juried, Visual Arts Center, Punta Gorda, FL,
June-July, 2012
Art Takes Times Square, Billboard Premiere at Times Square,
NY and website, June 2012
NLAPW - SW Florida Exhibition, Art Gallery, Cape Coral Library,
March 2012
NLAPW - SW Exhibition, The Art Gallery, Cape Coral Arts Studio,
January 2012

7th Annual Arists Registry Members Juried Exhibition, Gallery at Avalon, December 2011-January 2012

The Red chair Visits Public Art and Dance, Orange County Library, Winter Park. FL , December 2011

The Red Chair Visits Dance II, UCF Center for Emerging Media, Gallery 500, Orlando FL September 2011

The Red Chair Visits Dance I, Orange County Administration Bldg Exhibition Space, August 2011

Invitational Exhibition, CityArts Factory, Orlando, FL June - July 2011

First Annual Florida Juried Exhibition, Florida Museum for Women Artists, November 2010 - February 2011

6th Annual ArtistsRegistry Members Juried Exhibition, Gallery at Avalon Island, December 2010- January 2011

2010 Annual Juried Art Show, Osceola Center for the Arts, Kissimmee, FL May 2010

Women in the Arts 2010, Museum of the Americas, Doral, FL, March 7 - April 3 2010

5th Annual Artists Registry Members Juried Exhibit, Gallery at Avalon Island, Orlando, FL Dec 2009-Jan. 2010

Broward College Faculty Art Exhibition, Broward College Administrative Art Space, Jul-Sept 2009

Hispanic Heritage in America, Museum of the Americas, Doral, Fl Oct-Nov 2008

Seventh Annual Holiday Member Showcase, ArtServe, Ft Lauderdale Fl 2007

Summer International Exhibition, Museum of the Americas, Doral, Fl 2007

Mix It Up, a mixed media exhibition, ArtServe, Ft. Lauderdale, FL 2007

International Artists in California 2006, Latino Art Museum, Pomona, CA , December 1-30 2006

Summer International Exhibition, Museum of the Americas, Doral, FL, 2006

Tribute to Independence: Argentina and Colombia, Museum of the Americas, Miami, FL, 2005

Hispanic Heritage in America 2001, Latin American Art Museum, Miami, FL, 2001

Intuitive Art: The Artist as Shaman, Rosemary Court Galleries, Sarasota, Fl 2000

Fascinating Faces of Portraiture, invitational exhibition, ArtServe, Ft. Lauderdale, FL, 1998

Argentine Cultural Month, juried, The Florida Museum of Hispanic and Latin American Art, Miami, FL 1997

Presence of the Argentine Art, invitational exhibition, The Florida Museum of Hispanic and Latin American Art, Miami, FL 1996

BC Art Faculty Exhibition, Fine Art Gallery, Broward College, Davie, FL, 1995 - 98

Second Annual XS Best of the Gallery Exhibition, Art and Culture Center of Hollywood, FL, 1995

Herencia Hispana en America, invitational exhibition, The Florida Museum of Hispanic and Latin American Art, Miami, FL, 1995

Mujeres en el Arte, invitational exhibition, The Florida Museum of Hispanic and Latin American Art, Miami, FL, 1994

BC 1994 Art Faculty Exhibition, Fine Arts Gallery, Broward College, Davie, FL, 1994

Art Faculty Exhibition, Fine Arts Gallery, Broward College, Davie, FL, 1993

WCA Miami Chapter invitational Exhibition, The Art Gallery, Broward College, Pembroke Pines, FL, 1993

Broward College 1992 Art Faculty Exhibition, Fine Arts Gallery, Davie, FL, 1992

Women's Caucus for Art Invitational Exhibition, Bizarre Bazaar Gallery, Miami, FL, 1992

Women's Caucus for Art, Miami Chapter 20th Anniversary Juried Exhibition, Main Library Auditorium, Miami-Dade Public Library, Miami, FL, 1992

Broward Community College 1991 Art Faculty Exhibition, Fine Arts Gallery, Davie, FL, 1991

Works from the Permanent Collection, Art and Culture Center of Hollywood, Hollywood, FL, 1990/1991

Grand Opening Gala Celebration Exhibition, The Divine Feminine, Monterey, CA, 1990

Sky Art: Paintings in the Air, Art and Culture Center of Hollywood, FL, 1989

Invitational Exhibition, Broward Art Guild, Fort Lauderdale, FL, 1988

Faculty Exhibition, Fine Arts Gallery, Broward College, Davie, FL, 1988

Faculty Exhibition, Fine Arts Gallery, Browad College, Davie, FL, 1987

Expressions: The 6th Annual Competition and Exhibition, Art and Culture Center of Hollywood, 1986/87

Una Idea Mechanica, Initiated in Italy, traveled Europe and USA, 1986/87

Sky Art, Kassel Museum, Kassel, Germany, 1986

Connexus, South Regional Library, Pembroke Pines, FL 1986

BC Art Faculty Exhibition, Fine Arts Gallery, Broward College, Davie, FL, 1986

Connexus Environmental Sculpture Cooperative Project, Miami-Dade College, Miami, FL, 1985

Community Art Alliance 1985, Juried Exhibition, Hollywood Art and Culture Center, Hollywood, FL, 1985

Erotica, Juried Exhibition, Union Art Gallery, University of Wisconsin Milwaukee, Milwaukee, WI, 1984

BC Art Faculty Exhibition, Fine Arts Gallery, Broward College, Davie, FL, 1984

WCA Tri-State Juried Exhibition: Florida-Louisiana-Texas, Fine Arts Gallery, Broward College, Davie, FL, 1984

Aviary Art, Four Artist Exhibition, Fine Arts Gallery, Broward College, Davie, FL, 1984

Sky Art: Paintings in the Air, Invitational Exhibition, Art and Culture Center of Hollywood, Hollywood, FL , 1983

Hollywood Creates, Juried Exhibition, Art and Culture Center of Hollywood, Hollywood, FL, 1983

Art Faculty Exhibition, Fine Arts Gallery, Broward College, Davie, FL, 1983

Women's Vision, W.C.A. Juried Exhibition, Fine Arts Gallery, Broward College, Davie, FL and Philadelphia Art Alliance, Philadelphia, PA, 1983

Contemporary Women Artists of the Gold Coast, Invitational, Gulfstream Bank, Boca Raton, FL, 1982

BCC Faculty Exhibition, Fine Arts Gallery, Broward College, Davie, FL, 1982

The Community College Capitol Art Exhibit, Juried, The Capitol, Tallahassee, FL, 1982

Faculty Exhibition, Library Gallery, Barry University, North Miami, FL,1981

Inception, Juried, Jewish Community Center of South Florida, Miami Beach, FL, 1981

Greater Hollywood Creates, Juried, Art and Culture Center of Hollywood, Hollywood, FL, 1981

23rd Annual M. Allen Hortt Memorial Exhibition, Juried,The Museum of Art, Fort Lauderdale, FL, 1981

Channel 2 TV Juried Exhibition and TV Auction, Metropolitan Museum and Art Center, Coral Gables, FL, 1981

Local Color, Juried Exhibition, Grove House, Coconut Grove, FL, 1981

Whitney Counterweight 3, Invitational, Alain Bilhaud Gallery, New York, NY, 1981

Faculty Exhibition, Fine Arts Gallery, Broward College, Davie, FL, 1981

Invitational Show, Tropical Audubon Society, Miami, FL, 1980

Channel 2 TV Juried Exhibition and TV Auction, Miami, FL, 1980

Media Plus, Juried Exhibition, Lowe-Levinson Gallery, Miami Beach, FL, 1980

Southern Exposure: Selections by Women Artists, Juried Exhibition, Hanson Galleries, New Orleans, LA, 1980

SELECTED BOOKS AND EXHIBITION CATALOGS

Artblend Exhibition Catalog, Art Expo NY 2018, & Market Art & Design Hamptons NY 2018

Inspiration: International Art Book ContemporaryMasters Collection, 2017

Kyra Belan: Symbolic Magic, Exhibition Catalog, SBDAC Fort Myers FL 2017

Belan, Kyra. Divine Ladies in America, Astarte Books. 2016

Belan, Kyra. Earth, Myths, and Ecofeminist Art, Createspace, 2015

II Premio Internacional Don Quijote de la Mancha, Crisolart Galleries, Barcelona, Spain and Museum of the Americas, 2014

Aldrich, Jeffrey, editor. Art Takes Times Square, Signature Book Printing, 2013

Aldrich, Jeffrey, editor. One Life, Signature Book Printing, 2013

Aldrich, Jeffrey, editor. Art Takes Miami, Signature Book Printing, 2013

Carlos M. Guidicessi, editor. Contemporary Women Artists 2010, European Communities Artists Library, Barcelona, Spain, Dec. 2009

Carlos M. Giudicessi, editor. 100 Contemporary International Artists, European Communities Artists Library Press, Barcelona, Spain, 2007

Belan, Kyra. La Virgen en el Arte, Panamericana Press, 2007

Belan, Kyra. Art, Myths, and Rituals, Bent Tree Press, 2007

Belan, Kyra. The Virgin in Art: From Medieval to Modern, Barnes & Noble Press, 2005, 2007

Belán, Kyra. Madonnas: From Medieval to Modern, Parkstone Press, 2001

Belán, Kyra. Lucid Future, Aegina Press, 1999; CreateSpace 2012

Belán, Kyra. Earth, Spirit and Gender: Visual Language for the New Reality, Forbes, Inc., 1996, 1998, Thomson, 2001, 2003

Belán, Kyra. Site-Specific Works, chapter from Dorothy Gillespie, Radford University Press, 1998

Kyra Belán: The Floralia Series, Art and Culture Center of Hollywood, FL, 1995

Heller, Jules and Nancy G. Heller, editors. North American Women Artists of the Twentieth Century.Garland Publishing,Inc. New York and London, 1995

Broude, Norma and Garrard, Mary D. The Power of Feminist Art: Harry N. Abrahms Publishing Co., 1994

Belán, Kyra. Cover Art. The Latin Deli. Judith Ortiz Cofer. University of Georgia Press, 1993

Women's Caucus for Art, Miami Chapter 20th Anniversary Juried Exhibition. Main Library Auditorium, Miami-Dade Public Library System. Juror: Dorothy Gillespie. March 14-May 23, 1992

Orenstein, Gloria. The Reflowering of the Goddess. Pergamon Press, 1990

Kyra. Cover Art. The Line of the Sun. Judith Ortiz Cofer. University of Georgia Press. Athens, GA, 1989

Kyra. Cover Art. The University of Georgia Press Catalogue. Athens, GA, 1989

Wynne, Patrice. The Womanspirit Sourcebook. Harper & Row, 1988

Expressions! The 6th Annual Competition and Exhibition. Art and Culture Center of Hollywood. Juror: Judy Chicago.1986/87

Himnelsschreiber. Jonas Verlag. Harald Kimpel (Hg), 1986

Third Annual Miami Waves Experimental Film and Video Forum. Miami-Dade Community College, Miami, FL. Invitational. 1984

Erotica. University of Wisconsin-Milwaukee Union Art Gallery. Jurors: Jane Brite, Assistant Curator, Milwaukee Art Museum; Karen Savage, Associate Professor, School of the Art Institute, Chicago; Joan Semmel, Associate Professor, Rutgers University. Milwaukee, WI, 1984

Kyra. Foreword. Haitian Art of the 80's. Fine Arts Gallery, Broward Community College, 1984

Tufts, Eleanor. American Women Artists. Garland Publishing, 1984

Kyra. Foreword. Pottery Questions. Fine Arts Gallery, Broward Community College, 1983

Florida Visual Artists, 1982-1983. Fellowship Catalogue, Florida Department of State. George Firestone, Secretary of State. 1983

30th Anniversary Gallery Exhibition. Juried. Broward Art Guild, Fort Lauderdale, FL, 1982

24th Annual M. Allen Hortt Memorial Exhibition. The Museum of Art, Fort Lauderdale, FL, 1982

Kyra. Cover Art. Among the Ancestors. Judith Ortiz Cofer, 1981

Women's Vision. Juror: Dr. Paula Harper. Fine Arts Gallery, Broward Community College, FL and Philadelphia Art Alliance, Philadelphia, PA, 1981

American Artists of Renown, 1981-1982. Anne Avery, editor. Texas, Wilson Publishing Co., Gilmer, TX, 1981

Kyra. Illustration. The Native Dancer. Judith Ortiz Cofer. Lieb/Schott Publications, 1981

Inception. The Inaugural Event of the New Miami Beach Jewish Community Center. Juror: Dr. Eleanor Tufts. North Miami Beach, October 24 - November 29, 1981

23rd Annual M. Allen Hortt Memorial Exhibition. Juror: Donald B. Kuspid. Museum of Art, Fort Lauderdale, FL, 1982

Southern Exposure: Women Artists in the South. Juror: Dorothy Gillespie. Foreword: Donald B. Kuspid. Hanson Gallery, New Orleans, LA, 1980

Kyra. Illustration. Latin Women Pray. Judith Ortiz Cofer. The Florida Arts Gazette Press, 1980

Kyra. Magic Florida. Art and Culture Center of Hollywood, Hollywood, FL. September 9 - October 10, 1980

Media Plus. Lowe-Levinson Gallery, Temple Beth Shalom. Juror: Miriam Shapiro. Miami Beach, FL, May 5 - 24, 1980

SELECTED ARTICLES AND REVIEWS IN MAGAZINES

Artblend Exhibition Catalog, 2018

Cayla Childs, Sky Meets Sea, Gulfshore Life Magazine, April 2017

Carol DeFrank, Divine Women, Ft Myers Southwest Florida, March 2016

Mary Wozniak, Woman, Myth & Legend. Grandeur Magazine, October – December 2015

Filippo, Cathelijne. Lucid Future: a Spiritual Adventure. Paradigm Shift, issue 66 , May – August 2014.

Hall, Tom. News from the Atelier of Dr. Kyra Belan, Examiner, 05-23-14.

Hall, Tom. Local artist Kyra Belan included in UniteWomen.org national exhibition and catalog, Examiner, April 2013.

Bell Matuszewski, Barbara. Earth, Spirit, and Gender; Visual Language for the New Reality. The Pen Woman, February 2005

Belan, Kyra. Nancy Azara's Making Spiritual Practice of Making Art, Woman's Art Journal, Winter 2005, vol. 25 (2)

Belán, Kyra. The Art of Mary Beth Edelson. Woman's Art Journal, Fall 2003/Winter 2004, Vol. 24 (2)

Belán, Kyra. Art Portfolio: Digital Art. Magical Blend Magazine, November 2001

Benson, Mara K. Lucid Future by Kyra Belán. Magical Blend, 2000, no.69

Cox, James. A Penultimate New Age Novel. Midwest Book Review, February 4, 2000

DeBeer, Barbara. Earth, Spirit and Gender: Visual Language for the New Reality by Kyra Belán. Chrone Chronicles. Summer Solstice 1998, No. 35

Belán, Kyra. Discovering the Goddess Within. Of a Like Mind. Candelmas (Winter) 1998, vol. XIV, (4)

Weissman, Celia Y. Earth, Spirit and Gender: Visual Language for the New Reality by Kyra Belán. Women's Art Journal. Fall 1997/ Winter 1998, vol. 18 (2)

Cox, James. The Metaphysical Bookshelf. The Midwest Book Review, Internet Bookwatch. September 1997

Hakimi, Maxine. Kyra Belán, Priestess of Art. Pulp, January 1997

Wong, Sarah. Earth, Spirit and Gender: Visual Language for the New Reality by Kyra Belan. Magical Blend, August-September-October 1996, issue 52

Belan, Kyra. The Great Mother Archetype. Yoga Vedanta Journal. 1994, 3, (2). Also cover art and reproductions of artwork

Kyra. Cover art, illustration and brief bio. The Cathartic, No. 28, Spring/Summer 1992

Lauter, Estella. Women as Mythmakers Revisited. Quadrant XXIII:1,1990

Kyra. Cover art. The Cathartic. 1988, 20 (Spring)

Kyra. Art and profile. The New Renaissance. 1988, 22, (Spring)

Kyra. Cover art. On the Riviera. September 1987

Kyra. Goddess Images, Myths, and Symbols in the Art of Women of the Southeast. Southeastern College Art Conference Review. 1987, XI,(2)

Moore, Sylvia. Alternative Sources of Fundraising. Women Artists News, 1987, 12(2)

Kyra. The Magic Circle Series. Woman of Power. 1987, 6 (Spring)

Moore, Sylvia. Advocacy, Coalition of Women's Art Organizations. Women Artists News, 1987,12(2)

Kyra. Her Self. Hue Points, 1986,14(1)

Kyra. Cover art, illustration and profile. The Cathartic, 1984, 12

Gildar, Lisa. Male Nude: The Image is the Issue. Hue Points, 1983, 12(1)

Comini, Alessandra. The Hierarchy in Art History: Has it Changed After a Decade of Ferment? Women Artists News, 1983, 8(4)

Kyra. Censored: The Male Nude. Women Artists News, 1982/83, 8 (2)

Dressler, Kirt. The Newcomers: Up and Comers Among Them. The Best of Broward Including The Best of Lauderdale. 1981, Souvenir Edition

Goldberger, Carol. Florida's Feminist Artists. The Florida Arts Gazette., 1980, 4 (4)

Kyra. Male Nudes Still Draw Hostility in the Art World. New Directions for Women, 1980, 9 (6)

SELECTED REVIEWS IN PERIODICALS

Art Tour International, December 2018

Happenings Magazine, April 2017

Happenings Magazine, March 2014

Happenings Magazine, February 2012 & March 2012

Cogdill, Oline H. Local Book Reviews. Sun Sentinel, August 17th, 1996

Shulman, Sandra Carol. Mother Love: Artist Tracks the Mythology of Worshipping Women Since the Beginning of Time. XS Magazine, Special Eco Issue April 27, 1994

Kay, Julie. Earth Goddess Art Exhibit Opens at BCC South Campus. The Herald, April 14, 1994

Brown, Rene. Installation Praises Earth Divinity, Florida Flambeau, September 10, 1993

Happenings. Tallahassee Democrat. Friday, September 10, 1993

Fisher, Sophia M. Artist's Showcase. Fort Lauderdale News/Sun Sentinel, February 20, 1991

Higgins, Michael S. Exhibit Opens with Symbols of Peace. Hollywood Sun, January 25, 1991

Kohen, Helen L. It's Art Happening at the Zoo. The Miami Herald, March 27, 1987

Duke, Lynne. Art Show at Old Zoo Captivates Visitors. The Miami Herald, March 22, 1987

Blaylock, Debbie. Artist's Works Soar with Spirit of Freedom. Fort Lauderdale News/Sun Sentinel, June 30, 1985

Aver, James. Erotic Exhibit Shows a Different Blue Boy. Milwaukee Journal, August 6, 1984

Stanier, Carole. Fine Arts Gallery Offers Alternative: " Coatlique, Magic Circle VIII" by Kyra is a Good Example. Hollywood Sun-Tattler, June 15, 1984

Harper, Paula. Sky Painting: Good Idea, Bad Day. The Miami News, April 25, 1983

Stanier, Carol. BCC Faculty Displays Its Various Talents. Hollywood Sun-Tattler, February 11, 1983

Defino, Teresa. Exhibit Keeps Women's Art in Focus. Fort Lauderdale News and Sun-Sentinel, December 9, 1982

Kohen, Helen L. Broward's Eye on Reel Life: A Fine Video Update. The Miami Herald, November 12, 1982

Alioto, Susanne. Kyra: Giving a Shape to Magic Realism. The Miami Herald, February 11, 1982.

Lingner, Ellie. Regional Artist Maintains a Close Brush with Florida. Fort Lauderdale News and Sun-Sentinel, August 9, 1981

Mirrer, Lori. Magic of the Tropics Inspires Artist. Hollywood Sun-Tattler, September 5, 1980

Women to Watch in the 80's. Sun-Sentinel, January 15, 1980

Rayson, Kathy. Feminist Fights Bans on Her Art. Fort Lauderdale News and Sun-Sentinel, January 15, 1980

SELECTED PAPERS, PANELS AND LECTURES

Power, Resistance, and Gender Issues in the Arts of Women, CAA NY 107 Annual Conference, Panel Chair, 2019

Social Issues Art and Women Artists, CAA LA 106 Annual Conference. Panel Chair, 2018

Women and Social Issues Art, Panel Chair, CAA 105 Annual Conference, February 15 - 18, NY 2017

Technology and Women Artists, Panel Chair, CAA 104 Annual Conf., February 3-6, Washington, DC 2016

Women and Installation Art, Panel Chair, paper presenter, CAA 103 Annual Conf., February 11-14, New York, NY 2015.

Installation Art: Fine Arts, Digital Media, or Social Issues Art? panel chair; paper: Installation Art and Eco-Feminist Vision, SECAC, Sarasota, FL 2014

Winners of SECAC Artists of the Year Awards, panel presenter, American Beauty Series, SECAC, Raleigh, NC 2012.

Asian American Women Artists: A Postmodern Perspective. Panel chair. CAA 100th Annual Conference, February 20 - 23, Los Angeles, CA 2012.

Regional Women Artists: Exploring Nature, Spirituality, and Universal Order. panel chair, paper: Mother Earth, Thought Woman. CAA 2010 98th Annual Conference, February 10 - 13,Chicago, ILL, 2010

Mothers of Innovation III Exploring Mixed Media, New Media, panel chair, SECAC (Southeastern College Art Conference), Mobile, AL 2009

Mothers of Innovation II. Exploring Mixed Media, New Media., panel chair, paper: Mother Earth, Thought Woman: Installation, CAA 2090 97th Annual Conference, Los Angeles, CA Feb 25-28, 2009

Mothers of Innovation: Exploring Mixed Media, New Media: panel chair; paper: Mother Earth, Changing Woman: Installation, Performance, Video/dvd, CAA 96 Annual Conference, Dallas, Tx
February 20 - 23, 2008

The Sacred Feminine in Art and the Da Vince Code, chair; paper:
The Virgin in Art From Medieval to Modern, SECAC, Charleston, West Virginia, October 2007

Spirituality, Nature, and Social Issues: Installations and Experiments in Space, chair. Paper: Celebrating the Sacred Feminine: Installations, Digital works, Earthworks. CAA 95 Annual Conference, New York,
February 14-17, 2007. CAA Abstract

The Virgins, Madonnas, and Goddesses in Art., chair. Paper: Earth, Spirit, and Gender: Visual Language for the New Reality. CAA 94 Annual Conference, Boston, February 22-25, 2006.. CAA Abstract

Florida Women Artists: Re-defining the New Millennium, Panel chair. Southeastern College Art Conference, Little rock, AR October 2005

Women Artists in the New Millennium: Taming Postmodernism and the Printed Word, panel chair. Paper: Earth, Spirit, and Gender: Visual Language for the New Reality. CAA College Art Association 93 Annual Art conference, Atlanta, GA, February16-19, 2005, CAA Abstracts.2005

Women Artists as Interpreters of Socio-Political Issues of the Twenty-First Century, panel chair. Paper: The Archetypes of the Feminine and the Politics of Spirituality. College Art Association 92nd Annual Conference, Seattle, WA February 18-21, 2004

Installation, Performance and Ritual Art in the Twenty-First Century, panel chair. Paper: Artist as Shaman: Installation, Ritual Performance: Electronic Woman: The Computer and the Art of Southern Women, panel chair. Paper title: Lady Liberty and Other Archetypes. Southeastern College Art Conference, Raleigh, NC, October 29 - November 1, 2003

Woman as Divine: The Great Mother, the Goddess, and the Madonna, chair. Paper: Our Heavenly Mother, the Divine Madonna. College Art Association 91st Annual Conference, New York City. February 19-22, 2003. CAA Abstract

The Great Mother Archetype: Interpretations of the Divine Feminine, panel chair. Paper: Madonna From Medieval to Modern. Southeastern Art Conference, Mobile, AL October 2002

The Madonna and the Divine Feminine, panel chair. Paper title: Madonna from Medieval to Modern, College Art Association 90th Annual Conference, Philadelphia, February 20 -23, 2002.

The Virgin Mary as Redeemer, panel chair. Southeastern College Art Conference, Columbia, SC. October 24-27, 2001

The Artist as Shaman, paper. Southeastern College Art Conference, Columbia, SC. October 24-27, 2001

The Impact of Digital Technologies on College Level Art Programs, panel chair. Paper: Distance Learning, Digital Technologies and the Perplexing Issues of Copyright and Intellectual Property. College Art Association Annual Conference, Chicago, February 28-March 3, 2001

Books About or by Women Artists: An Important Contribution to Art History of the New Millennium, panel chair. Paper: Earth, spirit and Gender: Visual Language for the New Reality. College Art Association Annual Conference, New York, February 23-26, 2000

Books by or about Contemporary Women Artists: An important Contribution to Art History or a Passing Trend? panel chair. Paper: Artist as Author, an Emerging Tradition. College Art Association Annual Conference, Los Angeles, 1999

Eco-Spirituality, Nature, and the Artist as Shaman, panel chair; Paper: Shamanic Art in "Earth, Spirit and Gender: Visual Language for the New Reality." 1998 Southeastern College Art Conference, Miami Beach, FL, October 28-31, 1998

College Art Education for the Future Millennium, panel chair. Paper: Earth, Spirit and Gender College Art Association Annual Conference, Toronto, Canada, February 25 - 28, 1998

The Site Specific Multi-Media Installation as an Experiment in Creativity, panel chair. Paper: Goddess of the World: Site Specific Installation and Ritual Performance. 1997 Southeastern College Art Conference, Richmond, VA, October 23 - 26, 1997

Re-Visioning the Process of Art Education for the Future Millennium, panel chair. Paper: Earth, Spirit and Gender: Visual Language for the New Reality. College Art Association 1997 Annual Conference, February 12 - 15, New York, NY, 1997

The Eco-Spirituality in the Arts of Women of the South, panel chair. Paper: Earth, Spirit and Gender: Visual Language for the New Reality. 1996 Southeastern College Art Conference, Charleston, SC, October 24-26, 1996

Earth, Spirit and Gender: Visual Language for the New Reality, lecture. Is there Women's Art in the 90's? Roundtable discussion. Center for the Fine Arts, Miami, FL, July 13th, 1996

Visual Commentary on Culture and Nature, panel chair. Paper: A Personal Adventure into the Spirituality of Nature. College Art Association 83rd Annual Conference, Boston, MA, 1996

Exploring the Issues of Power, Gender and Spirit, panel chair.
Paper: The Flower as a Celebration of the Spiritual in Nature.
Southeastern College Art Conference, Washington, D.C., 1995
Celebrating Regionalism: Aesthetics, Cultural Diversity and the Art Issues
Outside New York, panel chair. Paper: The Exploration of Multicultural
Mythologies in the "Magic Circle Goddess Series." College Art
Association 82nd Annual Conference, San Antonio, TX, 1995
The Art of Dorothy Gillespie: A Spiritual Feast of Color, panel chair.
Paper: The Magic of Dorothy Gillespie's Site Specific Art.
Southeastern College Art Conference, New Orleans, LA. 1994
Art, Law and Social Values in the Nineties, panel chair. Paper: The
Effect of Sexist Attitudes on the Perception of Visual Artists By College
and University Students. College Art Association 81st Annual
Conference,February 17, 1994, New York, NY
The Shamanic Journey: Magic Circle Goddess Series (The Art of Kyra),
paper, The Thirteenth International Conference on the Fantastic in the
Arts, Dania, March 26, 1992
Art and Sexist Attitudes: Double Standard is Alive and Well in Higher
Education, paper, College Art Association 80th Annual Conference,
Chicago, IL, February 13, 1992
The Collegiate Art World: Education, Role Models, Law and Sexual
Politics, panel chair, College Art Association 80th Annual Conference,
Chicago, IL, February 13, 1992
Empowering Artists: the Role of Art Schools in Preparing Students to be
in Charge of Their Careers, panel chair, 79 Annual Conference of the
College Art Association of America, Washington, DC, February 21, 1991
The Great Goddess Archetype in the Works of Women Artists in the
Twentieth Century, paper, Southeastern College Art Conference,
The Atlanta College of Art, Atlanta, GA, October 26, 1990
In Quest of the Power of Myth, paper, Southeastern College Art
Conference, The Atlanta College of Art, Atlanta, GA, October 25, 1990
The Erotic Male Nude: A Mythical Metaphor, paper, The 11th
International Conference on the Fantastic in the Arts,
Dania, FL, March 25, 1990
The Illusion of Nature: A Journey into the Self, panel chair,
The 11th International Conference on the Fantastic in the Arts, Dania, FL,
March 22, 1990
The Berne Convention and Arts Legislation, panel chair, 78 Annual
Conference of the College Art Association of America, New York City,
NY, February 15, 1990
The Female Perspective of Sexuality and Power, panel chair, Southeastern
College Art Conference, 1989, Little Rock, October 27, 1989
Magic Circle Goddess Series: a Tribute to Female Spiritual Power, paper,
Southeastern College Art Conference 1989, Little Rock, October 27, 1989

Goddess Myths and Archetypes in Magic Circle Series, lecture,
Cape Cod Community College, Cape Cod, MA, March 24, 1989
The Diakosmos of Demeter and Persephone: a Drama of Life, Death and
Resurrection, paper, The International Association of the Fantastic in the
Arts 10th Annual Conference, Dania, FL, March 17, 1989
The Great Goddess as Symbol of the Mother Earth in Magic Circle
Goddess Series, lecture, Transformational Art Conference,
The Rim Institute, Payson, AZ, August 18, 1989
The Grass Roots Lobbying for the Arts, paper, 76 Annual Meeting of the
College Art Association of America, February 12, 1989
Goddess Chicomecoatl/Shakti: Magic Circle Goddess Series, lecture, Art
and Spirituality Conference, Payson, AZ, September 11, 1988
The Artist and the Law, panel chair, 76 Annual Meeting of the College Art
Association of America, Houston, February 12, 1988
Female Spirituality and Magic Circle Goddess Series, lecture, Women's
Alliance's Summer Workshops Camp, Nevada City, June 20, 1987
Great Goddess Coatlicue: Magic Circle VIII, paper, Southeastern College
Art Conference 1987 Annual Meeting, U. of Tennessee, Knoxville,
October 15, 1987
Male Nude: a Female Point of View, paper, Southeastern College Art
Conference 1986 Annual Meeting, U. of Alabama, Tuscaloosa,
October 31, 1986
Goddess Power and Revival of Feminist Mythology, paper, Southeastern
College Art Association 1986 Annual Meeting, U. of Alabama,
Tuscaloosa, October 30, 1986
Goddess Images, Myths and Symbols in the Art of Women of the
Southeast, panel chair, Southeastern College Art Association 1986 Annual
Meeting, U. of Alabama, Tuscaloosa, October 30, 1986
Goddess Isis: Magic Circle IV, video presentation, 72 Annual Meeting of
the College Art Association of America, February 24, 1984
Magic Circle Goddess Series, paper, 47 Annual Conference Mid America
College Art Association, St. Louis, October 27, 1983
The Erotic Male Nude, paper, 71 Annual Meeting of the College Art
Association of America, Philadelphia, PA February 18, 1983

DOCTORAL DISSERTATION, Florida International University, 1992
The Effect of Sexist Attitudes on the Perception of Visual Artists by
Community College and University Students

SLIDES/CD OF ARTWORKS BY KYRA BELAN: paintings, colored
pencil drawings, digital art, UCS (Universal Color Slides, publisher of
audio-visuals).

Selected Recent Lectures and Symposiums:

Kyra Belan. Divine Ladies book signing. Edison and Ford, Fort Myers FL. November 2016

Kyra Belan. Lucid Future book signing, Cape Coral Lee County Library, FL, December 6. 2014

Kyra Belan. Lucid Future book signing, Goddess I AM Healing and Arts Center, Naples, FL 2014

Kyra Belan. Lucid Future book signing, FWA, Orlando, FL Oct 2013

Kyra Belan. Lucid Future book signing, The Arts of Literature Bookseller, Cape Coral, FL, Aug.2012

Kyra Belan. The Art of Dorothy Gillespie, Florida Museum of Women Artists, Deland, FL 2011

Kyra Belan. The Virgin in Art, Southern Exposure: Literary Sampling, First Annual Book Fair, Broward College, February 2010

Kyra Belan. The Virgin in Art, Chattaqua Lecture Series. Coral Springs Museum of Art, FL. March 2009

Kyra Belan, director. Second Annual Seminole Art and Culture Symposium and Exhibition, Broward College, September- October 2008

Kyra Belan, director. First Annual Seminole Art and Culture Symposium and Grand Opening of Seminole Chickees, Broward College, September 2007

Professional Organizations:

CAA

CWAO (affiliated society, CAA)

SECAC

WCA

Selected Websites and Videos

Websites

Kyra Belán Website: https://www.kyrabelan.com
Ceres Gallery New York: http://www.ceresgallery.org/kbelan.html
artswfl.com: http://www.artswfl.com/artists/realist/belan-kyra/
dr-kyra-belan-berne-davis-and-barbara-b-mann
ftmyersmagazine.com: https://www.ftmyersmagazine.com/
FtM-edit.KyraBelan.html
Blink Art: https://blink.adcfineart.com/collections/kyra-belan
varoregistry.org: http://varoregistry.org/belan/index.html
Les Femmes Folles: https://femmesfollesnebraska.tumblr.com/
post/74937114653/kyra-belan-artist
fineartamerica.com: https://fineartamerica.com/profiles/kyrabelan.html
amazon.com: https://www.amazon.com/Kyra-Bel%C3%A1n/e/
B009ZEPR6O
parkstone-international.com: http://www.parkstone-international.com/
detail/2796/the-virgin-and-the-child/2#sthash.n0kTR76L.dpbs

Videos

Kyra Belan Ceres Gallery NY Solo Exhibition 2019: https://www.you-
tube.com/watch?v=xEuuP0u32-Y
Kyra Belan SBDAC Solo Exhibition 2017: https://www.youtube.com/
watch?v=JHYl-kD-Vi0
Artblend Kyra Belan Spectrum Miami 2017: https://www.youtube.com/
watch?v=7D6ENtSSEnQ
Kyra Belan at Spectrum-Miami 2016: https://www.youtube.com/
watch?v=ZcMZs9psV5I
Kyra Belan: Performance Art, Installation Artwork:
https://www.youtube.com/watch?v=8tF1rCddHeg
Kyra Belan: Installation Artwork: https://www.youtube.com/
watch?v=8I1QRTcue1U
 Dr. Kyra Belan - American Beauty: https://www.youtube.com/
watch?v=h7vJYLfucS4

Bio Sketch

Kyra Belán, BFA, MFA, Ed.D.

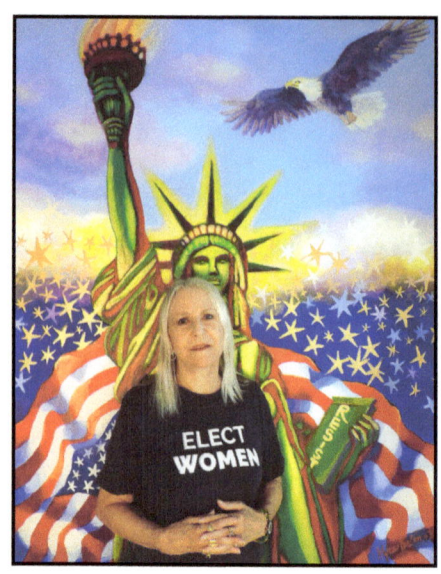

Artist, author, and art historian, Dr. Kyra Belán graduated from Arizona State University with a B.F.A. in Fine Arts, and from Florida State University with an M.F.A. in Visual Arts. Her Ed. D. from Florida International University is in higher education and art history.

Dr. Belán has had over 50 solo art exhibitions and has participated in over 100 group exhibitions. She has received numerous awards, including Who's Who in American Art, the Florida Achievement Award in the Arts; Women's Caucus for Art Florida Chapter Achievement Award; the Southeastern Art Conference Outstanding Artistic Achievement Award, University of Arkansas at Little Rock; Broward County's Women's Hall of Fame Outstanding Achievement in the Arts; and the Individual Artist Fellowship, State of Florida, Florida Arts Council. Her artworks are found in numerous public and private collections.

Author of several articles published in journals, Dr. Belán has also co-authored a book, Dorothy Gillespie, Radford University Press, 1998. She has written a novel, Lucid Future, CreateSpace Independent Publishing, 2014; and a book titled Madonnas: From Medieval to Modern, Parkstone Press, 2001 (English, German, and French). Fifth edition of her book, Earth, Spirit, and Gender, was published by Thomson; later edition, titled Art, Myths, and Rituals, was published by Bent Tree Press in 2009. Also The Virgin in Art: From Medieval to Modern, Barnes & Noble Books, New York, 2006, and La Virgen en el Arte, Panamericana, 2007; Earth, Myths, and Ecofeminist Art, CreateSpace 2015, and Divine Ladies in America, Astarte Books, 2016. Dr. Belán is included in The Power of Feminist Art, 1994, 100 Contemporary International Artists, publication of the Biblioteca de Artistas de las Comunidades Europeas, 2007; Inspiration:International Art Book, 2017 and other, and has written for Women's Art Journal and other periodicals..

Dr. Belán is the Otto Burkhardt Endowed Chair emerita professor of art and art history and founding gallery director at Broward College. Currently Dr. Belán is exhibiting her art nationally and internationally. She is a frequent presenter at CAA, SECAC and a frequent lecturer.

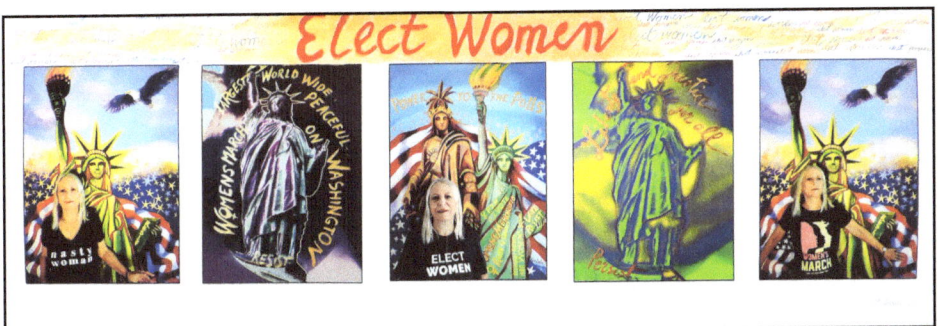

Elect Women
Mixed Media on paper 2019
24" x 72"

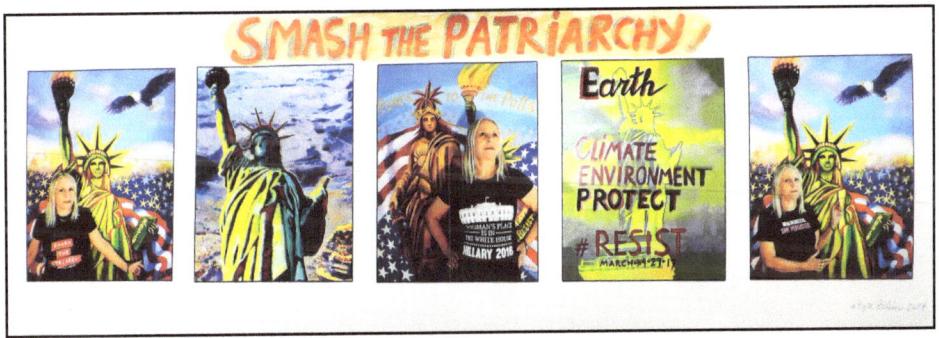

Smash the Patriarchy!
Mixed Media on paper 2019
24" x 72"